A Natural Act

A Natural Act

A Memoir

Jim McMullan

BearManor Media
2020

A Natural Act

© 2021 Helene Slack McMullan

All rights reserved.

No portion of this publication may be reproduced, stored, and/or copied electronically (except for academic use as a source), nor transmitted in any form or by any means without the prior written permission of the publisher and/or author.

Published in the United States of America by:

BearManor Media

4700 Millenia Blvd.
Suite 175 PMB 90497
Orlando, FL 32839

bearmanormedia.com

Printed in the United States.

Typesetting and layout by Helene Slack McMullan

ISBN—978-1-62933-788-3

Table of Contents

Beginnings 1

Stumbling into Hollywood 15

Universal Days 29

On My Own 43

A Starring Role...Finally 59

Image Section 75

Bread and Butter 93

The Bionic Connection 105

The World of the Television Pilot 119

Michael and Me 131

The Soaps 143

Featured Player 157

Actors As Artists 169

Commercials? Well, why Not? 183

Saved by the Bill 195

Epilogue 207

Chapter One

Beginnings

IT WAS 1955, one of those scorching July days that made you want to head for the beach and seek cool relief. But not me, not that day; I was in my parent's living room in Long Beach, along the south shore of Long Island. I was fingering my guitar, while an eight-year-old boy watched me and tried to do the same.

"This is the G chord," I said. "It's basic, like the C chord with the piano."

He held up his guitar to show me his fingering.

"Good," I said, and then I suggested he strum the chord a few times.

I was 19, and the boy, Jon Sholle, was a neighbor's son for whom I occasionally babysat.

His mother had asked me if I'd show him some guitar basics. "He's been obsessed with the guitar. That's the only music he wants to play or listen to." I told her I was hardly an expert, that essentially I was self-taught and knew only four basic chords. "But you *play*!" she said, and I admitted I'd worked those four chords into playing more than 100 songs, mostly of the folk variety.

That hot summer day sticks in my mind now because of what happened twelve years later. I unloaded my four chords on Jon Sholle that summer, then I went back to college. Within a couple of years, I made my way to Hollywood. I lost touch with him, but one day in 1967, a package arrived for me from his mother. How she got my address, I never discovered, but inside was an album. The cover photo had the caption, "Jon Sholle: World's Champion Guitar." He had won a national guitar competition at the 1967 Union Grove North Carolina Fiddler's Convention.

I smiled at the playfulness of the Gods because he'd achieved a career pinnacle and he wasn't old enough to vote.

All of that was a precursor because in the next 40 years, Jon's guitar skills allowed him to produce and be featured on several blues and jazz albums, to work with well-known musicians such as Bette Midler and Keith Carradine and even to appear on Broadway. That album so many years ago reminded me of those summer days, the eight-year-old boy and four simple guitar chords. It also confirmed my belief that talent is often hidden and does not require special training to become visible.

The town I grew up in, Long Beach, Long Island, was a beachfront community about 20 minutes from the heart of New York City, and it faced the wide expanse of the North Atlantic Ocean. Many commuted into the city for work, but others made their living from the sea, fishing or clamming or running tourist or party boats to those teeming, plentiful grounds that stretched along the south shore and up around Montauk Point, at the eastern end of Long Island. I've always loved the sea, and growing up so close to it gave me both an appreciation and a reverence for the purity and beauty of nature in its most uncomplicated form.

My mother and father had both been born in Scotland, though they hadn't known one another until they had met on a Long Island beach years after they had emigrated. My father, growing up in the rutty, industrial confines of Glasgow, had silently vowed to break away as soon as he was able. While still a teenager, he signed on to a Salvation Army tour which provided transportation to a new life in Canada. For him, this meant life as an indentured worker on a farm in the vast, flat but fertile lands of Saskatchewan where he would take two years to pay off his transatlantic passage and additional expenses he had accrued.

But it would allow him to escape the industrial hellhole that Glasgow had become and he reasoned the trade-off was well worth it. "I never looked back, Jimmy," he once said to me. "The future was always in front of me." It took him a while but eventually, he made his way out of Canada and into the US. In his mid-twenties, he landed work at one of those Long Island beach clubs with slatted white spires and weathered, shingled sides that an F. Scott Fitzgerald character attended. He worked on the beach and one day, he met my mother, who had taken an hour off from her maid's duties at the club to enjoy the sun.

Two Scots, far from their birth country, provided instant nostalgia for one another amidst an America flailing to emerge from the Depression. They bonded immediately and they knew what they had before them; the beach, the ocean, the American lifestyle was vastly superior to what they had left behind, and they intended to make the most of it.

Everything about where I grew up was water related, whether it was what we ate or where we went. And it went beyond summer time. Autumn and early winter along Long Island's south shore could be warm and beckoning. More than once I recall standing at the ocean's edge on New Years Day in just my bathing suit and a tee shirt.

When the weather changed, we'd walk the beach in January's swirling winds and find a protected spot for a driftwood fire. We'd do some surf casting in the spring when the bluefish were running. The beach was a steady companion for me and my friends, and it was like a personal playground. I loved it so much that in my later teens, I went through training and became a certified Long Beach lifeguard. I enjoyed the beach from sun-up to sun-down, day after day and got paid for it. I sat in that lifeguard chair and felt an integral part of the simple purity that nature offers.

At the same time, I had a yen for "building things" which usually meant I was in the garage banging away at some piece of metal or wood, trying to make it conform to an idea or an image I had in my head. I also became the house "fixer." My father wasn't very good with his hands, and I inherited a bit of talent for that sort of thing. So if the toilet handle needed adjustment or if the door jam needed resetting or if an electrical switch needed rewiring, I was the man.

I enjoyed doing that kind of thing, and it didn't hurt that I did it pretty well.

And I also loved art. I had a special sketchbook I carried around, which enabled me to follow my impulses when I saw or came upon something appealing. Then, I'd begin to draw.

One summer day when I was 15, I was sitting on the front lawn sketching sea birds careening through the air, and Maurice Sholle, who lived across the street and was Jon's father, came over.

He peered at my sketch for a moment. "That's good work," he said.

I thanked him, and he asked me whether I'd done any reading to develop my art work.

"I just like to draw," I said.

"I have a book which could help you," he said. I knew he was an industrial designer, though I had no idea what that meant. He invited me to stop over when I was finished, and when I did, he presented me with a beautiful book on design, *Vision in Motion* by Lazlo Moholy-Nagy.

"It's pretty basic," he said, "but it did help me when I was your age."

Suddenly, I had a direction for my undisciplined sketching. At the time, of course, I had no inkling there were so many forms of design work, from industrial to graphic to artistic design.

Since my neighbor was an industrial designer, I considered it, too.

College was in front of me, and I chose to enroll at New York University, just a short 20 minutes north on the Long Island Railroad. I was uncertain about what to study, but the industrial design idea stayed with me all through the college application process, and shortly after I started at NYU, I learned there was an affiliation with the Parsons School of Design in lower Manhattan.

Bingo, I thought, and I arranged to take courses at Parsons.

Looking back now, it was clear that attending both NYU and Parsons wasn't going to work for long. Design and making art was my overwhelming focus, and anything that took me away from that—such as my uninspired course work at NYU—was simply less important to me.

Then, fate intervened. I was home for the summer after my freshman year, when I awoke with a stabbing pain in my side. My mother took me to the emergency room at the local hospital where the resident in charge diagnosed appendicitis. "Your appendix," he said. "It needs to come out. You don't want it to burst."

By the end of the day, I'd had the operation and was resting quietly in my room. Standing by my bed was someone about my age. He smiled when he saw me looking at him.

"You're awake!" he said and introduced himself. He was an orderly and he was there to report any change in my vital signs. He wasn't a nurse, so his role was strictly as an observer.

Sticking from his back pocket was a sheaf of papers, which he pulled out and began to read. I asked him whether he had a lot of work to do.

"This isn't hospital stuff," he laughed, and he showed me the papers were applications to several colleges. "I'm applying to schools out west. I made a list and these have to be in soon."

He said he'd grown up around New York City and wanted to see what other parts of the world might be like. "Now's the time," he said, nodding to himself.

That night and part of the next day, I thought over what the orderly had said about spending his entire life around the New York metropolitan area. I had lived almost my entire life in the New York area, and while I loved living near the beach and had easy access to all forms of great artistic expression, it was like being in a playpen with walls. There *had* to be interesting stuff going on outside that playpen.

So the next day, a couple of hours before I was to be discharged, I found the orderly standing outside the recovery room.

"That list of colleges you're applying to. Can I see it?" I ran my eyes down the list and names like Wyoming, Texas, Kansas and Arizona sent my imagination flying: high mountains and wide prairies, great forests and roiling rivers, horses and wolves and elk and sheep so numerous as to be uncountable. Names out of adventure books and radio serials and Saturday afternoon movie shorts, like Wild Bill Hickok and Buffalo Bill and The Sundance Kid and The Lone Ranger and Wyatt Earp sped through my mind.

I handed the list back to the orderly. He must have seen something in my face because he patted my shoulder and said, "I'll help you put it together." Then he showed me what needed to accompany the applications and where to go if I had questions.

The more I thought of it, the more intriguing the idea became of going to school in the west. It would get me away from New York City. The country was vast and I had the feeling I would be at a frontier where life was simpler and rougher and more elemental, no longer the smooth-edged sophistication of New York with its wide avenues, tall buildings and surging crowds. I would be on my own among strangers in a land of broadened perspective, where the individual could be anything he wanted to be.

So I sent off several applications, and the first to reply was the University of Kansas, which accepted me for the upcoming fall semester. At that point, I hadn't mentioned anything to my parents. I was concerned they'd think me foolish to give up a life of certainty in New York for the uncertainty of a life where I had never been, among people I didn't know and studying at a university I knew so little about.

But they surprised me. When I laid out my plan to transfer to the University of Kansas, in Lawrence, my father asked just one question: "Is this what you *really* want to do?" I told him it was, that I was excited about going west. He glanced at my mother, then back at me. "Then follow your heart," he said, "and I wish you luck."

In the spring of 1955, I got off the train in Lawrence, almost expecting to see cowboys and Indians and had my first glimpse of the university. It sat on Mount Oread, with its peak at 1037 feet, the highest elevation in Kansas. With angular, gray stone buildings amid wide, green swathes of land, Lawrence looked clean and fresh and sturdy and substantial. From the first moment, I thought the university had a kind of beauty that reflected its wide-ranging educational mission. The architecture impressed me, as did the layout of the campus, and within days, I was feeling comfortable in my new home.

I chose an industrial design major that first year and began to polish up my guitar and singing skills. I had a decent voice and I began to play and sing at local gathering places around campus. It was a time when folk singing was sweeping the nation and artists like Burl Ives and Woody Guthrie and Pete Seeger were beginning to attract huge crowds. I had that 100 song repertoire I'd shared with Jon Sholle and my four chord approach. Within a couple of months, it got me some campus attention. The university radio station, KJHK, asked me if I'd like to do a weekly 15 minute music show, playing from my repertoire of folk music.

By this time I was comfortable playing before an audience, so I agreed. My opening night, before going on the air, I was reviewing what I intended to play with the station manager, when the studio door opened and this absolutely gigantic man filled the doorway.

"Looking for the station manager," he said in a deep voice.

I recognized him. It was Wilt Chamberlain, the seven foot tall basketball player from Philadelphia who was my first-year classmate at KU. His attendance at the university made headlines throughout the sports world. He dominated college basketball in the coming years as no other had done before him.

It turned out that Wilt Chamberlain wanted to be a disk jockey, and that evening he proposed to do a regular blues show over the air.

"I know this stuff," he said. "Been hearing it a long time."

The station, of course, was delighted, and they scheduled him for a half hour show each week right after me. By the third week, he and I were nodding acquaintances, and I would hang around to listen to him.

On the fourth week, during the break between our shows, he nodded at my guitar: "Always wanted to play one of those."

"I could show you some things," I said, thinking of my four big chords.

"Really?"

I nodded at this man who towered over me. "Next week, if you like."

And that began a weekly tutorial as I showed Wilt the rudiments of playing the guitar. I went over positioning the instrument, fingering it and learning the basic chords, and I marveled how an instrument whose size gave me all I could handle could seem so dainty and small in the delicate grip of this huge man. We worked each week throughout the semester, and by the end of the term, he had a good touch with each of my four basic chords. I encouraged him to move forward with his playing.

"Don't know," he said. "Got a lot going on." By this time, his basketball feats were being extolled on campus and across the sports world. KU had become a top-ranked basketball team, and there were interviews and appearances which limited his personal time. Eventually, he had to give up his campus radio show, but during our tutorials, he came across as both friendly and interested, a pleasant, down-to-earth giant of a man who wanted to learn to play the guitar.

After a year, I decided to confront my fear of math and change my major from industrial design to architecture. I enjoyed and felt comfortable with the general notion of designing and creating, but I wasn't sure where I fit in. My interest in building things, which stayed with me from childhood, made me want to create something concrete, something I could touch rather than some lines and circles and figures which might never be more than a blueprint for someone else.

I loved the cleaved stone architecture on the KU campus. The buildings were graceful yet substantial, but I knew in my heart that it wasn't the style of architecture I wanted to design. That little book, *Vision In Motion*, which I'd been given by Jon Sholle's father had planted in me the seeds of exciting, modern architecture. I'd imagine myself at the drawing table, dreaming up fantastic structures which would elicit gasps and approval from my professors.

By the early months of my junior year, I was settled on the architecture path; I consumed whatever I could find on the great architects, especially Frank Lloyd Wright, and I had dreams of visiting, perhaps even working at Wright's great architectural experiment in Arizona, Taliesin West.

One day, I got a call from Anne Runge, a girl I had been dating. She was a theater major, and she'd been trying for weeks to get me involved in an upcoming play. I resisted because acting on stage was something I'd never done.

This time she put on her most persuasive voice. "Jimmy, love, you know that play I've been so excited about?" She'd been on a high for days as the campus players were performing Eugene O'Neill's *Desire Under the Elms*, already a classic even though it had been first performed only 35 years earlier. Based on themes of incest, infanticide and retribution, it models the Greek tragedy of Phaedra but is set in early 1830s New England.

"There's a part that's just perfect for you," she went on. "You'd be great. Please say yes, please, please." The part was Eben Cabot, a debauched stepson of the cranky old patriarch of the Cabot family. Admittedly, when someone is that persuasive, it's not easy to say no. And I did like her a lot.

What have I got to lose? I asked myself.

"Okay," I finally said.

She told me I'd have to audition, which momentarily halted my enthusiasm. But she added, "I'll read with you, get you ready. Don't worry."

It went well and I got the part. It was my first time performing in a live play, and I enjoyed the experience. Many years later *Desire Under the Elms* reasserted itself in my life. Not long after I did the play, Paramount produced a movie version of *Desire Under the Elms* starring Tony Perkins, who played my role of Eben Cabot. The movie also starred Burl Ives and Sophia Loren, and I remember how excited I was to see a movie which showcased the role of Eben.

Walking to my seat, I smiled at my little secret; no one in the movie theater knew as much about the story line as I did and no one could rattle off the dialogue either from memory.

I noticed that Tony Perkins and I resembled one another. We were both lean-bodied, innocent looking and soft-spoken, but I was disappointed in his performance. I didn't think he captured the degenerate, amoral nature of Eben's character. He played him more positive than I had played him, more victim than victimizer. I remained excited as I watched though. I remembered almost all the lines from the stage play, and I quietly mouthed them to myself as they came out of Tony Perkins's mouth.

Nevertheless, I remember thinking that if this is what passes for professional acting, I'm sure I could do it at least as well. And it spurred me to go back on stage in other campus productions such as *The Most Happy Fella*, originally written by famed Broadway composer, Frank Loesser, and *Teahouse of the August Moon*, which had won the Pulitzer Prize for drama several years earlier.

In the course of my growing interest in acting, I started hanging out with several KU graduate students who also were involved in campus theater. Among them was Moses Gunn, one of the most interesting men I ever met. Of African-American descent, he grew up in St. Louis, one of seven kids, but when he was about 12 years old, the family had tragically split up, and he'd gone off on his own. For several years, he'd "ridden the rails," as he put it, traveling around the country on his own, living off the land. Somehow, by his late teens, he'd found himself back in St. Louis, where a former English teacher took him in and gave him a home so he could finish high school and attend college.

Years later, Moses and I met backstage at the campus theater, and by now he was studying theater arts in the master's program at KU. He had a strong, well-chiseled face and a deep, resonant voice, traits which years later would entice Joseph Papp to cast him as Aaron in *Titus Andronicus* in the well-known Shakespeare in the Park series in New York, for which Moses won an Obie Award. Still later, he performed the title role in *Othello* at the Stratford Shakespeare Festival.

The day we met backstage, I remember Moses gave me a penetrating stare, his face like stone. "You the one that rooms with Auggie?"

I nodded. He was referring to Augustine Kyei, my roommate who was from Ghana, West Africa. Auggie and I had known one another for more than a year and lived together in a campus co-op house. We paid $40 a month rent. He was studying architecture, too, his entire college experience underwritten by the Ghana Cocoa Marketing Board, and we had hit it off right away.

A week before, Auggie and I had gone to a local tavern about a block from campus to celebrate a high grade he'd received on a paper. I'd been in the tavern numerous times before, it was dingy and dark but comfortable, and the beer was cheap. As we started to sit at the bar, the burly bartender walked over and, pointing at Auggie, said, "You can't be in here."

"What do you mean?" I said, "He's a KU student, like me."

A look of mean narrowness crept into the bartender's eyes. "Who cares? He pointed at Auggie again. "He can't be in here. He's got to go."

I glanced over at Auggie, who gave me a pleading look, as if to say, it's not worth it.

Let's go.

"Look," I said to the bartender, trying to be reasonable, "he's an exchange student from Africa. He's studying architecture."

The bartender walked around the bar, and he reached to pick up something under the counter. "I said OUT! I'm not going to say it again."

I could see this was not a fight I wanted to pick. The bartender had each of us by 30 to 40 pounds, and he was pissed.

"All right," I said, nudging Auggie. "We'll go."

But I thought that somebody needed to hear about the incident.

I looked back at Moses and said, "It could have gotten uglier if we hadn't left."

Moses nodded. "We have to do something about this." He asked me straight away, "You in or out?"

This was 1959 when sit-ins and demonstrations on behalf of civil rights were developing across the southern United States. It was the time of the Freedom Riders and peaceful picketing and protesting. But little of it had reached Kansas, which, historically, had been a border state in the Civil War where the North and South had attacked one another. But Lawrence itself had been the center of the abolitionist movement in the West. That was a long time ago. But we knew, in the words of Bob Dylan, "the times, they are a-changin'."

And that meant in Kansas, too.

Moses suggested we form a civil rights council so we could make our collective points of view known. "It's something they've never had here, and Dr. King has shown us what happens when there's strength in numbers."

Moses must have assumed the civil rights call to action would have a greater response than it turned out. When we announced the formation of our council, only a handful of people showed up.

"It's a start," he said. "And you know what? We have a really good target to go after."

Moses meant the tavern where Auggie and I had been refused service. "We go after *them!*"

I looked around the group who had shown up. It was a mixed assortment of men and women, black and white. But it was representative of where we lived, and we all knew our mission was entirely justified.

"You ready?" Moses asked.

I shrugged, "Let's go."

And so the next day, ten of us appeared outside the tavern, carrying picket signs urging a boycott of the tavern. We held the signs high and waved at those passing by. We walked in a circle for two hours during the late afternoon so the cocktail crowd could see us. Once or twice, the tavern door opened and a face peered out, staring for a long moment and then retreating back behind the door..

The picketing went on day after day, never more than ten or twelve people, always peaceful, never blocking the tavern door but not relinquishing our share of the sidewalk, either. It took a while, but one day, several months after we had started, Moses called me, and he was excited.

"We got a deal," he said. "That tavern's going to serve everyone. No exceptions."

"We won?"

"We sure did. How's that for a story?"

Who would have guessed that the next time Moses and I were connected to each other would be 17 years later when we starred together, along with Don Johnson, also a KU graduate, in a television pilot, *Law of the Land*. From that point forward, Moses and I remained friends until his death in 1993.

Chapter Two
Stumbling into Hollywood

Even though I was enjoying myself in the campus drama productions and had made some good friends, like Moses Gunn, the KU acting scene was not my major interest. I really wanted to be an architect, I wanted to produce sweeping, awe-inspiring physical designs that would stand for generations. I wanted to create three dimensional art the way my private hero, Frank Lloyd Wright, had done, and no amount of acting or appearing on stage was going to get *that* done.

Early in my junior year, I answered an ad calling for an "apprentice" to work with a renowned local sculptor, Bernard "Poco" Frazier. He was already well-known for his artwork which graced public buildings throughout Kansas. Poco was commissioned to create stone art work and large murals to enliven the drab municipal buildings which marked Kansas' capital, Topeka. His sculptures had a traditionalist-Art Deco orientation, and he needed someone to help him create plaster molds for his clay-based designs, destined to find their homes in Topeka I loved learning his trade. Once the plaster was poured over the designs, it was allowed to dry, was removed and transported to the site where the art work would be displayed. Then, cement was poured into the plaster molds and left to harden. Afterwards, the plaster was removed and Poco's finished designs would take center stage.

As we worked together, Poco pointed out the nuances in his designs, and the challenges that were present when dealing with stone and cement. To this day, I think of him when I'm producing a piece of sculpture. He loved the work of Leonardo da Vinci and would occasionally quote him: "Where the spirit does not work with the hand, there is no art."

What working for Poco also did for me was to build my knowledge of and appreciation for designing in stone and other hard materials. Since architecture was where I was headed, understanding nuances in the materials I would be working with gave me a stronger feel for what I would eventually come up with. Stone, for example, needed "breathing space" anywhere that temperatures varied more than 50 degrees in a month.

Occasionally, I roughed out a piece of sculpture for myself, mainly from Poco's discarded leftovers.

He gave me quick reactions. "Top heavy," he might observe or "Needs more intercutting" or "lumpy-looking." Always, among his comments, he posed the arresting question,

"What are you trying to say, boy?"

When I started working for Poco in my junior year, I went to his studio two to three times a week. He was a busy man, and there was always more than one commission to work on. He had a young wife, Beverly, who would sometimes sit with us while we worked pouring plaster.

She and I became friendly, and one day she asked me how I got to KU from Long Island.

"Not many people from back east out here," she said.

I went through my story, emphasizing how I was looking for something new and different after a lifetime around metropolitan

New York City. "First time I saw the campus, the way it looked so clean and fresh, I knew I'd made a good choice."

"You sound like my brother," she said, mentioning him by name. David Glaze was a senior at KU. "Our family's from Los Angeles," she said. "We grew up there. And David's like you.

He wanted to try somewhere different." She and Poco had been living in Lawrence for several years, while he taught sculpture at KU. Then, her brother decided to leave the west coast. "One day, he called and a week later, here he was." She laughed. "You'd like him, I think."

How right she was about that. It turned out David Glaze and I were in the same psychology class, along with 35 others. A few days later, I introduced myself. "I work with Poco Frazier, and your sister thought we might have something in common," I said. "I think we're both in coast exile, you from the west, me from the east."

David had a generous smile, and we bonded right away. He made it plain, though, he had no interest in sculpture or in performing. "I'm a spectator, not a participant," he said with a grin.

"I think I know my limitations."

What I liked about him was his authenticity. He was genuine, never bragged about himself, had a ready smile and rarely took anything too seriously. "Best time to be alive," he said about beginning our third decades. "Young, single, energetic. Broke, of course."

We spent a lot of time together that year, and he was among the first to offer congratulations whenever I worked with the campus players. I remember his comment after I did *Desire Under the Elms*.

"You *were* that screwed-up character, that Eben Cabot. You really were."

I wasn't sure what to say because I couldn't believe I was *that* good; after all, I had had absolutely no acting training. It had been my first time on a live stage, and the whole thing had felt like a dream. Yet somewhere deep down inside, I had a distinct feeling: acting just isn't that difficult. I remember thinking the same thing when I saw Tony Perkins do my role in the film version of *Desire Under the Elms*.

At the end of the year, David graduated and I knew I was going to miss him. I asked him about his plans, hoping he might decide to stay around KU for at least another year.

"My mom wants me to come back to Los Angeles," he said. "She needs help." His mother ran a gift concession at the Los Angeles Gift Mart, and it was an active business. "She's all by herself," he added.

But wrapped up with my disappointment that David would be leaving was a feeling of excitement. It was the early 1960s, and John Kennedy was our new president. In 1961, he announced the formation of the Peace Corps, a place where young people like me might turn to find something more meaningful in life than a corporate career or enrolling in graduate school. It was a chance to travel and to live in a remote country we may never have heard of before, a chance to give to people in ways none of us had ever considered.

Many of us saw it as an adventure, as a chance to do something different, and when the Peace Corps recruiters appeared on the KU campus, a wave of excitement lifted us all. Three days after the recruiters came, I went for an interview. I hadn't thought through my plans for what was going to happen after graduation in a year from then. But the picture they painted was of helping others, doing it in exotic far-off places and in the name of the United States. They emphasized what a sense of fulfillment that could bring.

The recruiters told me they'd consider my application, but it might be months before I heard anything. "So many are applying," they said, and the program was still so new. They did say that if I was accepted, I'd go to the Dominican Republic because the program was already underway there. "We'll be in touch," they said, and as I walked out of the interview, I had the feeling I'd done something that could make me proud forever.

Periodically, during the next few months I'd check with the Peace Corps but the answer was always the same: you're on our list, but we can't make a commitment yet. Be patient and enjoy your college time.

It was frustrating, of course, because my senior year was coming to a close, and I still had not decided anything definite about what to do after graduation. I was involved with the campus theater, though Moses Gunn had moved on, and I was finding acting more agreeable than I would have imagined. But I reminded myself that I was going to have to get serious about things, once graduation came and went, and architecture was the career I had my eye on. First, I thought, was the Peace Corps. The idea that acting might fit in there or with architecture later seemed ridiculously implausible.

One day about a month before graduation, I got a phone call from David Glaze. We'd talked occasionally during my senior year, so he knew I was waiting to hear from the Peace Corps, and I knew he had been helping his mother at her wholesale gift store in Los Angeles.

"What are you going to do after graduation?" he asked.

I told him I might make a trek to Frank Lloyd Wright's Taliesin West complex in Arizona.

"And the Peace Corps?"

"Who knows?" I said. "It's been months now."

"What good would going to Arizona be if you wind up in the Peace Corps in a month or two?"

He had a point. Going to Arizona did feel like treading water and seemed purposeless.

"Why don't you come out here, stay with us for awhile?" he said. "You'd like my Mom, and she'd love the company. The Peace Corps can always contact you here."

I'd never been to California, let alone Los Angeles, I'd come as far as Kansas while seeking somewhere different, so why not all the way to the west coast? It would only be a for a little while.

So six weeks later after my KU graduation, I flew to Los Angeles, where David met me, and I settled in a spare bedroom at his mother

Arvella's apartment in Hollywood. Things were a bit cramped, but Arvella was gone almost every day setting up her booth at the Gift Mart, and David and I roamed around Hollywood. I was no movie buff at that time, though I'd heard about major Hollywood landmarks such as the Brown Derby or the Hollywood Boulevard Walk of Fame. One day, we were sitting in the car overlooking the Hollywood landscape. I remember the sun was beginning to set and the sky was turning from blue to pink. Below, you could see the gray remnants of valley smog, but up high the air was clear and the colors were vivid.

David said, "You ever given any thought to doing some acting? You were really good in college."

I reminded him I was waiting for the Peace Corps to come through, and that I wanted to be an architect.

"But right now, this moment, you're not committed to anything, right?"

I nodded, not sure where the discussion was headed.

"You ever hear of the writer, William Inge?"

"Why would I?"

"He's kind of a big deal. He writes plays, and with you in college theater, I thought…"

I reminded David that I was not an actor, not a *real* actor, anyway. "I'm going to be an architect," I reiterated.

It turned out that William Inge was from Kansas, and David had met his agent a couple of times at festivals where Arvella had a booth. The agent said Inge was interested in helping anyone from Kansas who wanted to get into show business. David listed some of Inge's successful plays: *Picnic, The Dark at the Top of the Stairs, Bus Stop, Come Back Little Sheba*. The agent had underscored to David how serious Inge was in helping anyone from Kansas. "He really means it!"

At that moment, William Inge was staying in Hollywood, writing the screen play for a new movie, *Splendor in the Grass*, which would star Warren Beatty and Natalie Wood. "I can introduce you to see William Inge," David said, mentioning he'd do it through the agent. "The guy's a serious Kansas booster," David grinned, "and you're a Kansas Jayhawk. He writes plays you act, what's there to lose?"

I'm *not* an actor, I wanted to say, but looking at David's eager face, and hearing the excitement in his voice, I hesitated. It might be fun, meeting a real writer, someone actually famous.

"Okay," I said, "why not?"

By mid-morning the next day, David had set it up. He stressed the Kansas connection to Inge's agent, and the fact I'd acted in college. Then he spoke to Inge himself, and Inge said he could give us a few moments only and to come up to his rental house in Beverly Hills early that afternoon.

"He's really doing us a favor," David emphasized, "so you don't want to overstay your time."

David dropped me at Inge's door early that afternoon. "I'm not coming in," he said. "You theater types need your alone time."

I punched his shoulder lightly. "How many times do I--"

"Right. Architect. Peace Corps." David laughed. "I'll be back for you in two hours."

Inge's rental was a large private home with a swimming pool and some lush, manicured greenery. He greeted me warmly, a slender man, shorter than me, with a lined face and sharp, focused eyes.

"Come in," he said. "Always pleased when someone from Kansas makes his way out here." He suggested we go sit by the pool, and the atmosphere seemed relaxed, pleasant. I had no agenda beyond enjoying the moment, and we began to talk about ourselves. He described the movie he was working on, mentioning he was excited to be teaming up with Elia Kazan, the director.

"He's got a great touch," Inge said. "Instinctive, almost."

He asked me about my admittedly thin theater experience, and then I mentioned I had worked with Poco Frazier.

"Oh, I know him," Inge said. "Great artist, I love his work."

Suddenly, I was aware of his eyes scrutinizing me, measuring me.

"You've got a nice look," he murmured, softly, "an interesting look…"

I could feel myself get warm, embarrassed.

He patted the seat next to him. "Come on, sit over here. Let's be comfortable."

I wasn't sure what to do when he added, "How about going for a swim. No one's around. You don't even need to put on a bathing suit."

I shook my head and blurted out, "I-I don't think so. I'm not much for swimming." Of course, he didn't know I'd been a life guard and had grown up around the beach and I sure wasn't going to clue him in.

My digging my heels in seemed to cool him down because soon, he was talking about being in Hollywood. "I come out here to work," he said, "but I don't like the Hollywood atmosphere, the busyness of it. I love Kansas. It's quiet. It's refreshing. If I were you, I'd think long and hard about getting involved out here."

I shared his feelings about the more tranquil nature of Kansas, but I'd grown up fifteen minutes from New York so a city atmosphere was something I was used to. And anyway, I would be off to the Peace Corps soon and then develop an architectural career, so acting and settling down in Hollywood just wasn't going to happen. I was sure about that.

We talked for a little while longer, and then I heard David's car come into the drive. Inge stood up and held out his hand. "Always glad to touch base with someone from Kansas," he said, and for a long moment, he gave me that focused stare. "What if I introduce you to my agent?"

You look great. You've acted. You have a 'look.'" He chuckled to himself. "They like that out here."

I shrugged, not sure exactly what he was getting at but I wanted to keep the conversation as cordial as I could. "Sure," I said, "why not?"

A few moments later, I climbed into David's car and we headed out the driveway. "How'd it go?" he asked.

I really had no answer because I wasn't quite sure what had happened, except that I felt a bit unnerved by Inge's attentions. "Nice guy," I said and tried to leave it at that.

The next day, I got a phone call from someone named Marvin Burt. He introduced himself as William Inge's agent and said that Inge suggested we get together. That was quick, I thought, then realized this sort of thing was no big deal. I had the "look," whatever that was.

Probably hundreds of others had it, too. Burt asked me to come over to his office in Hollywood.

Three hours later, I was ushered into his glitzy corner office at the top of a Beverly Hills high rise and was face-to-face with a Hollywood character out of central casting: fast-talking, slick, tanned, cold blue eyes that raked me with sharp intensity. He spent five minutes asking about my limited theater experience, adding, "No television or movie stuff, right?"

I nodded, and he sat back, eyes on the ceiling, slowly picking his teeth with a fingernail.

A few moments went by. Finally, he leaned forward, nodding. "I'm going to call over to MGM because they're looking for new contract people."

And ten minutes later, I was ushered out of his office. An appointment at MGM was set for the next day/ I still wondered just what I was getting into.

Marvin Burt told me to ask for Zina Provendie who was the head of casting for MGM.

She was a tall slender woman with a mass of black hair in ringlets set off by dangling earrings.

She looked me over casually.

"You're Marvin's guy?" she asked.

I nodded and she handed me a sheaf of papers. "Here's a short scene from an old sci-fi movie. Learn it and come back here next week and perform it for us." I noticed the scene called for two characters, and I wondered who the other one would be. "That's up to you," she said.

"Find someone. Just be back here next week."

Fortunately, David had an actress friend, Jainie Palmer, a perky blonde actress about my age, who had come out from the Midwest, looking to build a Hollywood career. She agreed to do the scene with me and we rehearsed it vigorously for the next few days. At that point, the Peace Corps still hadn't come through and I was beginning to wonder if it ever would. That was still my goal, but I had to admit that dipping my toe in the acting world was getting to be a lot of fun.

The next week, Jainie and I went to the MGM casting offices and Zina was waiting for us, along with three other people. They took us into a vacant office which had several desks and some open floor space.

"Okay," said Zina, "let's see what you can do." And for the next fifteen minutes Jainie and I did the scene before an audience of four people.

I had no idea how well we did. All they did was thank us and send us on our way. I'd been quite nervous and I hoped it hadn't shown. But the next day, Zina called me. "We liked you very much. All of us did. So, how about doing a screen test?"

I had no idea what that was but my mind was swirling.

"I'm sending you a scene from a movie that's currently in pre-production here," Zina went on, explaining that they were testing not only me but another actor, and they would be using one of their contract players, Joan Staley, to play the scene with me. It turned out Joan Staley had been *Playboy* magazine's November 1958 "Playmate of the Month," a sexy, bubbly blonde who turned out to be easy to work with. "Get together with Joan," Zina said, "rehearse with her, get the scene down and then we'll have you do it before the cameras."

They tracked Joan down to an MGM sound stage where she was watching production set up for a television movie. A half an hour later, Joan walked into Zina's office, a big smile on her face, hand outstretched.

"I like you already," she said

At the time, I didn't have the experience or knowledge to understand why I felt so relaxed the moment she arrived. Later in my career, of course, I understood the feeling, that we simply "clicked." There was a subtle symbiosis between us that made it seem we had worked together numerous times before.

It's not a feeling you get very often, especially in the acting world. But other actors know what I mean when I mention it because at one time or another, we all experience it.

Joan said she knew of an empty office down the hall where we could rehearse and she led us there. The scene was from an MGM movie then in pre-production: *Ride the High Country*, and the stars were Randolph Scott and Joel McCrea. My character was a young gunfighter, meeting Joan's character for the first time. I'm supposed to be coming on to her while she's playing coy, and the tension in our differing attitudes was supposed to create a romantic spark.

Joan laughed after the first run-through: "I *know* how to be coy," she said, "but sometimes it's a waste of time."

"You're more a tell-it-like-it-is type person?

"You could say that."

But she played the coy heroine well and I quickly got in the spirit of the scene. I liked the script. My character's name was Heck, and at some point in the movie he would get to ride a camel, which I thought was very cool. We ran the scene through again and again, and I could feel myself growing quite comfortable, not only with Joan but with the scene and my place in it.

Then, a strange feeling came over me, something totally unbidden, unexpected. Was it possible, could someone, me, for example, do this kind of thing for a living? Could I become a serious, full-time actor?

As we took our places to go over the scene again, Joan smiled at me warmly, and her words have stayed with me ever since: "You could be quite good at this, I think."

If my head had been spinning because of my own thoughts, now it began to swirl like a dervish.

One of the production assistants stuck his head in the door, asked if we were finished rehearsing and told us Zina wanted us to go on the actual set and do the scene. "They're waiting for you over there," he said.

Joan and I exchanged looks. "You'll never forget your first screen test," she said, and we followed the assistant down to the sound stage.

The set contained an outdoor backdrop with an actual corral and a live horse stomping and nickering alongside. Sprinkled about were lights and several cameras.

"Hold it," an assistant producer whispered, as we were about to walk on the set. He put his finger to his mouth and pointed. Another couple had entered the corral and were readying for a scene. "Their screen test, too," he said, motioning that we step back and wait for them to finish.

It turned out the male actor was someone named Ron Starr, who happened to be a close friend of the director, Sam Peckinpah, and who had never acted in a movie before. The woman, playing the same role as Joan Staley would play with me, was Mariette Hartley, who later went on to a successful Hollywood career. It was obvious she was on the cusp of big things. She had the "look," that indefinable quality of physical and character attractiveness actors must have to succeed. I recognized it in her, just as William Inge had said he recognized it in me, but to this day, I'm at a loss to define it further. As the old saying goes, I may not be able to tell you what it is, but I sure know it when I see it.

We watched them do our scene and one thing was clear: Mariette Hartley was a pro, a strong, talented actor who would add solid authenticity to her role. Unfortunately, the same thing couldn't be said about Ron Starr. He was not a trained movie actor and it showed. He didn't sound "real" in the part, his vocal inflections and mannerisms seemed contrived, and there was an unnaturalness to his physical movements.

"I don't know about him," I whispered to Joan Staley.

"He's Sam Peckinpah's buddy, so..."

She didn't have to finish. Who you know works in Hollywood too, I figured.

She tapped me on the arm. "You'll do the scene much better, I can tell."

A half hour later, they called us onto the set. Sam Peckinpah, tall, red-haired, mustachioed, gravel-voiced, told us what he wanted to see: me, sexually aggressive, sure of myself, clearly attracted to Joan, who would be coy, yet interested, firm and self-assured.

I had heard of Sam Peckinpah. At the time, he was one Hollywood's most in-demand directors, even though it was well-known he also suffered serious personal drug and alcohol problems. His films were sparked by their vivid scenes of violence and action. There were some who believed he deliberately got high prior to directing a scene so it could spur the authenticity of the action he wanted to see. Among his many credits are violent films such as *The Wild Bunch*, *Pat Garrett and Billy the Kid* and *Straw Dogs*.

But with us that day, he had little to say beyond what he expected our characters to show.

And in an hour we were finished. Peckinpah shook our hands, thanked us and walked off the set.

I turned to Joan. "Strange guy."

"A Hollywood legend to some, I guess."

"You think we impressed him?"

She shrugged, "He's tough to read."

"I enjoyed doing that role," I said.

"I wouldn't hold my breath. He wants Ron Starr on the movie."

She told me he and Starr were buddies and he was doing his friend a favor by casting him in the movie. "But," she added, "you did a good job on the test. You came over well."

Years later, after I'd established a respectable acting career, I was working on an MGM television series called *Beyond Westworld*, and one of the script editors walked up to me on set 29 and said, "Got a surprise for you." It turned out he had found a copy of my screen test with Joan Staley while he was digging through the MGM archives for something else.

We went into the editing room and played it back. I have to admit, in spite of what Joan had said, it was pretty bad, pretty embarrassing. You could tell there was something there, something the casting people must have seen, but the acting itself, wasn't much. I realized in that moment that in spite of relying on what I considered my natural instinct when it came to a role, I must have developed acting skills I wasn't aware I had developed.

That, of course, was far into the future. For the moment, I was content. I had had a screen test. Joan Staley, an experienced actor, had told me it went well. I knew I could act better than some, like Ron Starr, who would get a role due to who he knew. And still, I was waiting to hear from the Peace Corps, and planning on a career in architecture.

Chapter Three

Universal Days

A FEW DAYS later, I got a call from the agent, Marvin Burt.

"Your screen test," he said. "Revue Studios liked it. They want to see you." He told me to ask for Jere Henshaw and Monique James, vice presidents of casting and talent, respectively, "They're waiting for you," he added. Then he gave me a verbal pat on the shoulder. "Good luck, kid."

My head was spinning. A few weeks before, I had graduated from college, casually wondering how my life was going to play out. Now, I had met William Inge, Marvin Burt, taken a Hollywood screen test. Kansas and that flat yellow-green farmland suddenly seemed far, far away.

At the Revue Studio gate, they directed me to a large bungalow. "Casting and Talent" was on the sign in front. Inside, I was escorted to a corner office where two people were waiting.

"Jere Henshaw," said a trim, well-dressed executive, shaking my hand. Standing next to him was a short, pleasant woman. "This is Monique James," Henshaw said, and she smiled warmly, urging me to sit down.

I didn't know it at the time, but Monique James had discovered both Warren Beatty and an actor who would have an impact on my later career, Robert Redford. Her eye for talent was legendary.

"Our people are impressed with your screen test," Henshaw said. "With training and proper career management, we think you could become a star."

"We don't say that to many people," James added I stared at them. A star?

"But you'll need to pay your dues," Henshaw said. "That means beginning with bit parts and working your way up. It won't be easy and it takes time."

They explained I would become a "contract actor" for Revue Studios which meant I would sign a seven-year contract and be cast in shows produced on the lot. I would be paid $350 per week but every six months they had an option of canceling my contract. Many actors had started out like this, they said, including Doris Day, Lana Turner and Cary Grant. It was a way to get experience and build up an audience.

Two days later, I got a call to appear on my first show. At the time, westerns were popular, with *Wagon Train*, *The Virginian*, *Laramie* and *Tales of Wells Fargo* getting high ratings week after week. They slated me for a new show, *Frontier Circus*, about a traveling circus in the old west. John Derek and Chill Wills, a couple of experienced actors, played the leads, and I had only three lines, but it was a start. I knew I wanted to be in this business, and my eagerness to learn must have shown because one of the cast members, Richard Jaeckel, asked me if this was my first show.

I remembered Jaeckel from *The Sands of Iwo Jima*, a popular World War II movie. We chatted for awhile and discovered we had both been born in Long Beach, Long Island, though ten years apart. He gave me a tip I've never forgotten: "Always read with someone *before* you do a scene," he said. "Let someone *hea*r you read your lines."

Then, he urged me to understand what my lines meant in the context of the scene. "It's more important to know the life of the scene than it is to know your lines. If you know the story situation, and you forget your lines, you can always make up something so you don't screw up the other actors."

I found a small rent controlled apartment right across the street from the studio front gate, and I decided to learn everything I could about the business. As a contract actor, I had the run of the studio, sound stages, back lots and all. I'd get up in the morning, say hello to the guard at the front gate and go to the commissary for a cup of coffee. There was a celebrity dining room next to the commissary, with waiters and a special menu. That's where I'd see people like Rock Hudson and Alfred Hitchcock have their morning meals. I told myself that one day I'd be in there at my own table, too.

I looked on it all as my personal playground, and I would wander from sound stage to sound stage, watching, listening and learning. There was always something going on, films at various points of production, people hurrying from place to place, the sounds of music and vehicles and shouting.

One day, a sound stage guard I knew waved me over.

"You don't want to miss this one, Jimmy," he said, nodding for me to go through a doorway. Inside was Marlon Brando and they were shooting *The Ugly American*. I'd heard he would write his lines out and pin them around the stage outside of camera range so as he worked, he could recite the lines, instead of having to memorize them. This way, he felt, they'd come across as fresher. He was in a close-up with another actor, and sure enough, there was a piece of paper pinned on the wall just out of camera view. For a moment, I thought they were rehearsing, but then I noticed the director standing outside camera range, watching intently while the camera whirred. Each time the camera moved away from Brando, even for a few seconds, he would sneak a look at that piece of paper on the wall.

About this time, Revue Studios was sold and became Universal Studios, and I began to get cast in Universal shows, especially the westerns. There was *Laramie, The Wide Country* and, *Wagon Train*, among others. I was meeting and working with some fascinating people. In 1962, I met Slim Pickens who was a regular on *Wagon Train*, and we hit it off right away. A big man with a down-home casualness that exuded warmth, he had been a rodeo clown when he was discovered. The studio people interviewed him, threw him a couple of lines which he threw right back at them, and they loved it.

I asked him how he felt about acting.

"Are you kidding? I'm no actor." He gave a rollicking laugh. "They give me lines once in a while, but I keep fooling them. Actor? Me?"

Slim Pickens dismissed the idea that someone could learn to act. For him, it was all about being yourself and making others believe. I was so new to all this, but when Slim boiled his approach down like he did, I really related to it. I'd never taken acting classes, never studied with an acting teacher, never had a stage career. Like Slim Pickens, I thought maybe I could "fool" them, too.

When I heard about a big feature film being shot in the back lot, I'd go and watch. One day, I found out Spencer Tracy and some comedians were shooting the comedy classic *It's A Mad, Mad, Mad, Mad World*, and I stopped in at the sound stage. Tracy wandered over, curious to know who I was because there was no one around but cast and production people. To my surprise, he sat down next to me and held out his hand, introducing himself. I told him how much in awe of his work I was and how excited I was to meet him.

He made a pained face and said, "Let's not talk about me. Let's talk about you." I told him I was a contract player, which impressed him as there weren't many under contract at that time.

"No one really knows where acting can take them," he said. "I'm doing a comedy here, and it's something I don't do very often." He gave a wry smile and shook his head. "But they're paying me a lot of money, and I just wanted to do something a little different. Kind of a change of pace."

I could see he really didn't want to talk about acting, but there was one question I couldn't resist. "I read that when you were asked about your acting technique, you said, 'Show up on time, know your lines and don't bump into the furniture.'"

"Naw," he said disdainfully. "Someone made that up, but it's pretty good advice. I just like to keep it simple, be there and listen."

It brought me back to Slim Pickens whose approach was as simple in its own way; Give me some lines and maybe I can fool you.

Soon, I got my first chance to work in a television pilot (a stand alone episode of a television series used to sell the show to a network). It was called *The Plainsman*, and it was to star Robert Culp as Wild Bill Hickok. Monique James had called me about it. "You ready for something bigger?" she asked, then added that I would have to audition because several other actors were also being considered.

"What's the role?"

"Young Buffalo Bill. You'll be playing against Bob Culp's Hickok."

At the time, playing Buffalo Bill carried no special significance beyond its immediate bounce to my bank account and a push to my career. But if I could have looked 35 years into the future, to 1998, this initial connection with Buffalo Bill certainly would have seemed ironic.

I was the last actor to test for the role, and when I arrived on the set, there was Robert Culp. He looked weary, and his face showed what he must have been thinking: Oh, Christ, here comes another one.

Still, I looked up to Culp. He was such a seasoned pro. When we started to run the scene, I could tell he liked something about the way we interacted. The weariness seemed to fall from his face. And when it was over, he tapped me on the shoulder, nodded and smiled, "Nice job, kid."

I realized later Culp had a big say on who would get the part, and the next day he himself called me. "Congratulations and welcome. You've got the role. I think we'll work well together."

Once we began shooting the pilot, Culp's influence over the show was pervasive and occasionally disruptive. "I want perfection," he said, again and again. He argues with the wardrobe person over the hat he was to wear or whether he was to use suspenders. He fought with the makeup person over the type of blush that went on his cheeks or the shadowing around his eyes.

He was very specific about what was right for him, and I looked on, wide-eyed and somewhat uncomfortable. I didn't like the idea of arguing with someone and then having to work with them.

We shot the pilot in 12 days and by the end, we were pretty excited about it. I read up on the Young Buffalo Bill character, and I felt I'd come to know him intimately. But a month after we finished, Monique James called to say Universal was not going forward with the series. No reasons were given, but we suspected it might have been too expensive to produce. That was confirmed when she added, "We'd like to turn the pilot into a feature film because we *do* like what we have. We're going to add a half hour, same story line, same characters, only with more depth. And we'll shoot it in Mexico.

They renamed it *The Raiders* and it played as a television movie. At the time, I hadn't digested "the Culp approach," which demanded perfection, perfection, perfection. But after I saw the finished show, I was struck by the most obvious incongruity: There was Young Buffalo Bill, short hair combed back, neatly dressed, almost a dandy, when he should have been rough hewn, long-haired, messy, a true creature of the Wild West. If I had been Robert Culp, I would have growled, "Ridiculous! Make me scruffy. Get the grease out of my hair."

I also learned a painful lesson in my first feature film. In Hollywood's Old West, characters lived dangerously and frequently, they had to fight or jump or fall. I was young, athletic, sure of myself, and there were a couple of stunts I insisted on doing alone. One of them involved a barroom fight and while filming, I fell awkwardly and bloodied my knee badly. And I suffered shooting pains from knee to hip so bad that I could barely walk.

"Stay off your feet for a couple of days," the doctor ordered, and the director, right there, listening. Nothing was said, but I knew I had screwed up the director's shooting schedule.

"We'll shoot around you," he muttered, an edge in his voice, and he walked away shaking his head.

An old-time stunt man, Lenny Gear, gray-haired, wiry, with leathery skin, caught up with me when I returned to work.

"Here's a tip for you kid," he said. "Stunt men like me get paid to do these stunts for you. In that bar fight, you looked really bad, and it's probably going to have to be reshot. We know how to do these things without getting hurt, and we make you look really great because from a distance, who's going to know it's not you throwing his body around? And guaranteed, you won't piss off the director by having to reshoot the scene."

All of a sudden the light went on in my head. The stunt man does his thing on the long shot, and then I come in and they recreate some close shots of my face so when they cut those together, it looks as if I'm the one doing the fabulous stunt.

"Sounds good to me," I said. Lenny invited me to come out to his ranch in the San Fernando Valley the next weekend, to show me how stunt men got trained to do the various tricks they did with their fists and their horses. It turned out to be excellent training for me, too, because Gary Combs, one of Lenny's best stunt men, was there, and we hit it off right away. During the next few months, Gary worked with me so I learned to throw punches that looked real.

He showed me how to handle horse jumps and trick riding exercises and I grew very comfortable in the saddle. At the time, the studio continued to cast me in westerns, so the training helped with my roles. Gary Coombs did all of my stunts.

But I wasn't totally out of the woods when it came to stunt work. Occasionally, a director would say, "I want you to do this stunt," and

I remembered that abortive bar fight which screwed up the shooting schedule. So, I'd respond with "It'll look a lot better if you let Gary do it." Bob Culp would have been happy with me saying that to the director, because it would be a step toward "perfection."

Mostly, the director would shrug and walk away. But one time, on a *Wagon Train* episode, I played a preacher and my co-star was Clu Gulager, an experienced western actor. The scene was a campsite in the mountains, and the director said to me, "You're reading a bible, and Gulager walks up and slaps it from your hands, growling, 'I don't want to hear any more of that bible-thumping stuff!' You begin to fight, wrestling him to the ground. It ends quickly as people pull you apart."

I looked the director in the eye, remembering Bob Culp and how he controlled his role and Lenny Gear and how stunt men made us all look better. "Not a good idea," I said, "Someone could get hurt."

The director didn't back down. "What are you, a pansy? Come on, let's get on with it!"

He said this loudly enough for most of the cast to hear. I was still new to the business and unsure of the career consequences of saying no to a director. By now, everyone on the sound stage was looking at us, and the director stared at me, waiting. I realized I wasn't holding winning cards; I could be easily replaced, and who'd ever hear of Jim McMullan again?

So I did the stunt. The director slapped me on the back and I didn't get hurt. But I learned to pick my fights, literally and figuratively, carefully.

Even though Universal was casting me in westerns, they also wanted to see how I'd perform in a non-western role.

"Let's check your appeal with different audiences," Monique James told me. Frankly, as long as I was enjoying myself in front of the camera, I hadn't paid much attention to the details of who was supposed to be watching me. I felt I was riding a crest of a magical wave that would never end.

"Whatever you want," I said to Monique James, open to any suggestion.

At that time, the networks were producing hour-long, non-series dramas, and one of the most successful was *Alcoa Premiere*. Universal cast me in "The Masked Marine," about a soldier learning humility the hard way. I played opposite James Caan, and he and I bonded almost immediately. He was from the Bronx. I was from Long Island, but we were both New Yorkers.

"Where you from on the Island?" he asked.

"Long Beach, south shore."

He let out a laugh. "We used to go there in the summers." From that point on, we were friends.

At the time, Mel Brooks and Carl Reiner had made a splash with their ingenious "Two Thousand Year Old Man" sketches, and Jimmy and I decided to lighten things up on the set and try our hand with the format. We'd listen to the records and re-create the routines. He played the Brooks role, I played Reiner, and while still on break, we called the cast and crew together and started in.

As every actor knows, there are times when you improvise and it simply "works." There's really no way to explain it. You sense you're floating high above problems and storm clouds. You feel strong, confident, in control, and you know it'll continue.

That's the way the first Brooks-Reiner sketch with Jimmy Caan went. The watchers laughed with us and at us, again and again, as we fed one another the crazy lines. We only stopped when the director, a blunt man named James Sheldon, broke it up by growling, "God damn it! We're already 40 minutes behind shooting schedule!"

As it happened, Jimmy and I continued to do the routines during breaks, and the cast and crew urged us on. What we didn't know was that the show, itself, was falling behind schedule, going over budget, and the producers were looking for a scapegoat. One day, I was called into an office. There sat James Sheldon, and two grim-faced producers.

Sheldon began, "I've watched you guys joke around on the set for weeks, and you're causing us to fall behind schedule."

"We only do the routine during breaks," I protested.

One of the producers chimed in. "You're messing around too much. The cast and crew are getting sloppy. *That's* what's causing problems."

I didn't figure to win this battle, so I kept quiet while they warned me to cut out the joking around and pay better attention to cues and direction.

"We have a god damn schedule. Remember that!" Sheldon added.

Over the next year, Jimmy and I saw a lot of one another. We bought motorcycles and rode all over Southern California together, up the coast to Santa Barbara, down to San Diego and east to Riverside. We were young and free-spirited and having fun.

One day, after we'd finished "The Masked Marine," he called to say he was working on a big new movie, *Lady In a Cage* starring Olivia de Havilland. I knew Jimmy's training had been as a "method" actor and he said, "I'm going to the Los Angeles County Zoo to study a live jaguar because that's the image I feel this character needs." I told him I'd like to go along because method acting was something I'd heard about but had never seen up close. Just like Spencer Tracy, I was comfortable doing it the "natural" way. Yet, I was curious about the method technique.

We walked up to the jaguar cage, and Jimmy sat on a bench facing the animal.

"Give me a couple of hours," he said, and he turned into a statue, body forward, eyes glued to the sleek, spotted killer who paced back and forth. The animal did seem to fit the image of his movie character who was to kidnap Olivia de Havilland, put her in a cage and torment her.

Somehow, he hoped to get the feel of the way the jaguar moved so he could transfer it to his acting.

Did it work? He thought it did because when he came out of his self-induced trance, he had a big grin. "I'm buying!" he announced, as we headed out to eat.

By this time, our careers were moving in different directions. Jimmy wanted to concentrate on movies while I was happy with television work. Our joint rides grew fewer and fewer until I knew it was time to move on. I wished Jimmy good luck and waited for Universal to decide where to cast me.

Jimmy's method approach did cause me to plumb my own attitudes about acting. My gut feeling was that I had an innate sense of what acting was all about, and I didn't need the crutch of "transcendence" that method actors used. To me, acting was a natural thing, the way Spencer Tracy had described it. Some might say I rejected the method approach because I feared digging deeply into myself, while others might accuse me of laziness. But I liked the natural approach. It was fun, not painful and without all that introspection and angst some method actors experienced. I knew I could find a way to relate to any part, but it would have to happen intuitively.

I got a call from Jere Henshaw at Universal. "Looks like you're on your way to Oregon," he said, "The studio's putting together a feature film, and we've cast you in it." The role was the middle son of a Virginia farmer during the Civil War. The farmer wanted nothing to do with the war, but when his younger son was kidnapped by the Confederates, the family mobilized to go after him.

"They're calling the movie, *Shenandoah*, though it's being shot in Oregon."

"Who am I working with?" I asked.

"Jimmy Stewart's the lead."

Jimmy Stewart! I could hardly believe my good fortune.

Later on, I also discovered that Jimmy Stewart was my kind of actor. He'd never studied acting, never had much live theater experience, never worked on Broadway. Basically, he was an intuitive movie actor. It all came from his heart. He'd listen to the muse and then he'd perform.

He, like Tracy, was a hero of mine. He was quite amazing in the way he could instantly pick up his role. One minute he'd be having a conversation about visual art. Then he'd get the call to play a scene where one of his kids is shot, and suddenly he was full of anger, slipping into the role so effortlessly.

This was to be my first feature film, and I was excited. In order to recreate the Virginia countryside, they used matte artists, something that digital enhancement has now replaced. In those days, digitizing anything was at least a quarter-century away, so the matte artist would be the scene creator and appear on the set with an easel. Shooting was out of doors, of course, so the artist would watch the action unfold, say a group of wagons moving along a trail, And then he or she would place a matte on the easel and paint in a farmhouse, perhaps a grove of trees, too, as well as impressive looking hills to vividly bring out the Shenandoah Valley background. Then, the matte was put in front of the camera lens, and the images of the wagons would be blended with the images produced by the artist. The entire scene would seamlessly depict the Virginia countryside, even though we were shooting in Oregon.

I was on the set a couple of days when I first met Jimmy Stewart. He was sitting at a prop table playing chess with one of the assistant producers. I'd learned to play from my father, and I stopped to watch. After a while, he made a move and quietly uttered, "Checkmate!"

"Nice," I said.

He looked up. "You play?"

I nodded, "A little."

By this time, his opponent had stood and muttered something about finding a cup of coffee so Stewart motioned to the empty seat. "Got half an hour before next call," he said, looking at me closely. "You play my son, John, right?" He held out his hand, and I introduced myself.

That started a regular chess game that lasted throughout the entire shooting of the film. We developed a pleasant relationship over the chessboard that made working with him easy and fun. One day, I discovered that Jimmy had an architecture degree from Princeton.

"Same degree here," I said and told him how much I enjoyed designing and creating art.

He looked at the people milling around the set and put on that gentle smile.

"Don't know how well I'd have done in the design trenches," he said, "but I did enjoy studying architecture." He asked me whose work interested me most, and I mentioned Frank Lloyd Wright.

"What a talented man," he said. We talked about design philosophy and he mentioned his friend and fellow film star, James Mason, had also studied architecture. "Funny about that, isn't it? Architecture to acting. We probably aren't the only ones, either."

I told him I also painted, and he nodded. "Artists and acting. I know something about that, too."

"One sort of feeds the other, don't you think?" I suggested.

"I know a lot of actors who like to paint," he said, mentioning his friends Edward G. Robinson, James Cagney and Ralph Bellamy. "In fact," he chuckled, "at this moment, Claudette Colbert is finishing a portrait of my wife Gloria."

"How about you?" I asked.

He motioned with his hands dismissively. "Well, sure, I paint, but." He laughed. "My work's not for public consumption. I'm pretty lousy, actually."

But he did enjoy talking about art. He and some of his friends, especially those who were serious about their painting, would meet and have lively discussions about what they were working on. "I'm always surprised how many actors enjoy painting, and you know what? A lot of their work is pretty damn good."

The subject didn't come up again while we were shooting the film, though we continued our chess games and often compared our early architectural training. But, unknowingly, Jimmy Stewart had planted a seed in my mind that would flower almost thirty years later. Actors as artists. I wondered how many I could find?

Chapter Four

On My Own

AFTER *SHENANDOAH* **WRAPPED** up, I felt a heady sense of accomplishment: I'd worked alongside and learned from a legend, Jimmy Stewart. I'd been complemented for a professional attitude and a "solid" performance by the director, and I knew the movie had all the makings of a hit.

But as the weeks went by and nothing in my life changed, I found myself wondering if this would lead to something bigger? I was now about two years into my Universal contract, and the parts I was being offered were minor supporting roles, limited in the number of lines and overall impact on the story lines. It felt like I was treading water and I was getting impatient.

Hadn't Jere Henshaw and Monique James talked about making me a star? I understood all this could take time, maybe a lot of time, but after two years, I thought there would be some bigger roles.

I could see it wasn't happening. I spoke to Marvin Burt about it. "You'd think after working with Jimmy Stewart..." I began.

Marvin held up a hand. "It isn't like the guy has a magic wand. You're on your own out here, my friend. You, me, even Jimmy Stewart."

Marvin added that just because I was a Universal contract actor was no guarantee of anything. He reminded me of what the contract said: "It may say it's for seven years, but really it's a series of six month contracts, and they have the right to drop you at the end of each six month period." He shrugged. "Just the way they do things."

I mentioned my growing displeasure with the roles I was getting and the lack of interest I perceived from the casting people. Marvin nodded, a rueful smile on his face. "Two years ago, you were the 'shiny new thing,'" he said. "Now you're not, and someone else is." He said it had nothing to do with my acting ability. "They're just used to you, I guess." He said it happened all the time, a momentary "crush" on an actor by the casting department until the next exciting performer came along. But that didn't mean I had no future as an actor, only that we'd need to think about going in a new direction.

There are many reasons why an actor leaves his agent, but in most cases, it's due to long periods of no auditions and no work. The actor usually arranges a meeting with the agent to discuss the sticky situation, and the agent, suspecting the actor is ready to jump ship, will make up excuses as to why he isn't being sent out to casting sessions and the agent will promise to work harder. These meetings are always painful.

In the beginning, there's the honeymoon phase, when the agent tells you he has great hopes for your future and puts forth extra effort to find you work. It's a sweet ride when the agent continues sending you out to auditions, and you are lucky enough to keep working. But as it happens, a new actor who is your age and type signs with the agent and suddenly, the honeymoon is over. The agent now has a new piece of meat to peddle.

I sensed this was where my conversation with Marvin was headed. "You mean walk away from this?" I asked, upset, spreading my arms to include the entire Universal property.

Marvin knew I loved being at the studio and walking around the property, watching various projects at different stages of production. I had an apartment right across from the studio, and it was so easy to spend my days at Universal and soak up the atmosphere, even if I wasn't currently cast 47 in anything. I knew all the guards and most of the prop and scenery people. After two years, the Universal lot really felt like a second home.

The reluctance I felt must have shown on my face because Marvin nudged me on the shoulder and pointed skyward. "Come on," he said, "up there, that's where the future is. You need to fly, Jim, higher than where you are." He said it was time for me to go "freelance," to go out on my own, choose my own roles, make my own future. "You won't be sorry," he added.

A big, empty pit formed in my belly. It felt like I was cutting an umbilical cord to a place where I had felt safe and comfortable. Now, I would go into an entirely different world, a dog-eat-dog world, where I didn't have the security of a regular paycheck.

"You really think I could do this?" I asked.

"It's time, Jim," he responded.

And within a week, I had my first freelance acting gig. It was a single episode role on *Dr. Kildare*, a weekly one hour MGM television drama that profiled the problem-filled life of a young doctor at a fictional metropolitan hospital. Though this was in he early 1960s, the character of Dr. Kildare had actually been created 25 years earlier by MGM and had, at that time, become a popular movie series. A quarter of a century later, the television show resurrected the character, and just like its movie ancestor, it attracted a solid audience. Richard Chamberlain played Dr. Kildare, and Raymond Massey played his superior and moral compass, Dr. Leonard Gillespie. Guest stars from Jack Nicholson to Lauren Bacall appeared regularly on the show, but there would also be roles for lesser known actors like me, and this was how Marvin Burt sold me on going freelance. "Lots of shows out there, Jim, they're always looking for good talent. You fit well."

My part on *Dr. Kildare* was a doctor who had a drinking problem and tried, not so successfully, to hide it. What really sold me on doing the role was who would be my love interest: Angie Dickinson, a woman I had always admired. What a presence she had. She lit up the place when you were around her, a gorgeous, talented actor. She played a nurse to my doctor, and for the show, we were in a relationship, though my character's drinking got in the way. In one scene, for example, she came to my apartment, only to find me drunk. She stormed at me, saying I shouldn't be a doctor if I couldn't control my drinking, and eventually it was the drinking that broke us up on the screen.

I was delighted to be working with Angie, and she must have felt something for me, as well. Twenty years after that one show, my wife Helene, and I were at the Academy of Motion Picture Arts and Sciences building on our way to a screening. We walked into an elevator full of people and there was Angie. She cried out, "Jim! My old boyfriend!" And we gave each other a big hug as the amazed onlookers wondered what the hell was going on. We hadn't laid eyes on one another since the *Dr. Kildare* show, but she still looked gorgeous and she still had that indefinable "magic" that I remembered from all those years before.

It took a week to shoot the *Dr. Kildare* episode, standard for this type of one hour show, and I never did figure out how my agent got me the role, especially opposite the talented Angie.

But when it was over, I knew I'd taken a big step. I was out on my own. I felt validated about my decision to leave Universal and my agent and I were in synch. A week after the *Dr. Kildare* episode aired, I got a call from Marvin Burt.

"I loved what you did on *Kildare*," he said, adding I might be a "natural" for the doctor shows. "The networks are keen on them right now, so I've sent a copy of your *Kildare* work to the *Ben Casey* show." It was a competing medical drama. He said they were looking for actors like me to build a younger audience. Marvin and most of the other high-level Hollywood agents belonged to a "breakdown service," which regularly listed all movies in production, at what stage of production, the characters that needed to be cast and contact information. The agents would determine where their clients might fit, then submit resumes and photos, and follow up with phone calls and even personal visits. Agents sought to create strong, personal relationships with casting people so their clients would receive more than a casual examination. This could lead, as it did in Marvin Burt's case, to the development of mutual respect between agent and casting department, based on the reliability of the agent's judgment on who should be cast for what roles.

An agent's ability to navigate successfully through the chaos of the casting scene is underscored when you realize there could be as many fifty or sixty agents submitting their clients' material for a single role. An agent whose credibility had not been established to the casting director would not fare well here.

I was fortunate to draw Leo Penn as the director for my appearance on *Dr. Kildare*. He had been an actor before he became a director, and as it turned out, his son was the now famous Sean Penn. I remember young Sean visiting the *Dr. Kildare set*. He couldn't have been more than five years old. Leo introduced me, put him on my lap, and we watched that day's action together.

He didn't say much, and it was apparent he felt comfortable with the television studio scene.

When we were finished for the day, he jumped down, gave me a big smile and hurried off to find his father.

What separates the merely good directors from the great ones? I've always considered Leo Penn in the latter category. He was an actor before he started to direct, and it was apparent that he understood the way actors felt about learning lines, rehearsing too much or being micromanaged. Leo never overexplained how he wanted an actor to do his or her part. He trusted the actor to know the lines, and he exuded respect for the actor's ability.

He was far different from others I had to deal with. Some directors simply want to control everything, from where the actor stands to how the actor handles dialogue, and in some cases, how the actor utters *every* syllable of dialogue. To me, that tends to ruin everything. There's a freedom that comes when the actor feels trust from the director, when the actor *knows* he or she won't be controlled by the director and is simply "let go" to perform as he or she sees the role developing. Perhaps later, after the performance, the director might suggest tweaking a line or two differently, or getting a bit more emotion into a given utterance, but directors like Leo Penn let the actor perform as the actor saw the role before suggesting any changes.

A couple of days after Marvin sent my *Kildare* tape to the *Ben Casey* show, they called and asked that I contact the MGM casting department to set up an audition.

"They're looking for a new doctor character to work under the lead doctor, Ben Casey," Marvin said. "A kind of sidekick, younger, less experienced." Vince Edwards played the lead and I would be reading for the role of Dr. Terry McDaniel, a young neurosurgeon. I had never met Vince Edwards and knew little about him, other than he was from New York City and had turned the Ben Casey role into a success.

The next day, I went over to the MGM casting department, expecting the audition to be set up and the casting people to be waiting. That was the way it had been at Universal.

Imagine my surprise when I walked into the MGM casting office and found a dozen or so other actors milling around, along with agents and production people, everyone talking at once and no one seeming to be in charge. It turned out we were all there to audition for the Terry McDaniel role and it would be a plum gig because it would continue for eight episodes and possibly more. It offered an assured source of income for a while, and every actor wanted the security of that.

Finally, I had my audition, and immediately, I felt right at home with the scene I was given to read. I felt confident talking with the production and casting people, who asked me about my acting background. I felt really at ease playing a doctor and acting in a hospital scene, and it must have showed because three days later, Marvin called with words every actor loves to hear: "You got the part and it's an eight week contract." What I didn't expect was what happened after that. My euphoria over getting the part dissolved like a papier-mâché house in a rainstorm by the end of my second day on the set.

I had walked into a hornet's nest. The atmosphere was about as unfriendly as it could be.

Some members of the cast carried grudges against other members of the cast. No one cared about hiding his or her feelings. And Vince Edwards, the star, wanted to control everything.

Edwards, an Italian-American, had been born in Brooklyn and had grown up there. He had been an outstanding swimmer, recruited by Ohio State University and had been part of a championship swim team. Acting, however, was what he preferred, and after college, he had attended the American Academy of Dramatic Arts and then fashioned a B-movie career through the 1950s, particularly in film noir productions. It was his role as Ben Casey, however, that made him a star, and when I met him on the set, I was startled by his cold demeanor, by his flat eyes that projected no warmth whatsoever, and by the fact he really wasn't a very good actor.

I recall interacting with him on numerous scenes, and when the director yelled "cut," he'd walk away without a word, as if I wasn't even there. There'd be no follow-up, no further relationship, and it made me feel as if I was a piece of the furniture rather than a breathing member of the cast.

And there were the two heavily muscled characters who showed up every day and hung around the periphery of the set. Vito and Mickey were their names, and it became clear right away they answered to Vince Edwards. A couple of days into my first week's rehearsal, I asked one of the assistant producers why they were there.

"Ask Edwards," he said. "They're part of his contract." Both had been professional boxers, thick-chested characters with ugly, scarred faces who never said much but were always looming. Vito was the taller of the two, and he sported a pair of ears that looked as if someone had chewed on them. Mickey was more blocky, square, and he had the coldest gray eyes I'd ever seen.

"They're like Vince's bodyguards," the assistant producer went on. "They protect him."

From what, I wanted to ask. A runaway sound boom or perhaps a prop guy with a hangover? "What's to be protected from on this set?"

He responded with a shrug. "Who knows?"

From the outset, it was clear Edwards ran things with an iron hand, and he had the majority of control over the set, even when it came to the director. There were times when we'd finish a scene and he'd say, "I don't like the way that went. We need to do it again." And the director would comply. Or Edwards might say, "I want to change how this scene ends." And just like that, we'd have to change the ending. He'd never let us forget he was the star of the show, and he wanted everything to revolve around him, even when rewriting or changing something meant another actor might lose lines or on-camera time. It's *my* show, he seemed to be saying. We'll do things *my* way.

Marlyn Mason, a pretty blond actress from California, played my love interest, a nurse, on the show, and we got along well. Not only was she talented, but she was easy to work with, and by the end of our first rehearsal, I was feeling as comfortable working with her, as I had with Joan Staley during my initial audition days. Often, Marlyn and I would find an empty office down the hall from the set where we could rehearse and prepare for our on-camera work. A couple of times, as we walked off the set together on our way to rehearse, I noticed Vito or Mickey eying us, sometimes tracking us until we were out of sight. I didn't pay much attention, figuring it was Marlyn, a most attractive young woman, who was the attention magnet. But one day, midway through my eight week contract,

Marlyn and I returned to the set after rehearsing down the hall, and Mickey was waiting, his cold, gray eyes flat and hard. He jerked his head in the direction of an empty corner of the set and walked over to meet me there. I sensed Vito coming up behind me, and suddenly I had Mickey face-to-face and Vito at my back.

Then, I heard Vito's harsh words in my ear. "There's something you need to know, fella."

Mickey eyes gripped me like a vise. "Listen good, here. Listen *real* good," he mumbled quietly.

"You don't want to get too friendly with her," Vito warned. I knew he was talking about Marlyn. "She's Vince's girl. You got that?"

Every set always bulges with rumors, often about relationships between the actors, and this one was no exception. I'd heard numerous comments about how Vince Edwards considered himself a "ladies man" and would often hit on female co-stars, sometimes with success. But I'd never heard about him and Marlyn, and to this day I don't know whether Vito had it right. One thing I did know, however. I didn't want or need to face down either of these thugs who watched over Vince Edwards's social life. No way was this going to be some kind of macho contest. So, for the remainder of my eight week contract, Marlyn and I maintained a pleasant but restrained relationship away from the cameras.

And I'm quite happy I never worked with Vince Edwards again.

After my time on *Ben Casey*, I felt good about my acting prospects. My credits were building, and I'd just finished a multi-episode, featured player gig on a highly rated show that counted millions of watchers each week. In the weeks after the show, I'd be walking along some street miles from Hollywood or Century City, and there'd be a sudden look on a stranger's face, then a stare. I could feel the stranger's eyes on my back as the space between us grew.

I could sense what was in the stranger's mind: I know him from somewhere, seen him somewhere. I'm not saying I'd base acting success on who and how many people recognized me publicly. That's a fool's conclusion, Yet, I have to say I enjoyed the momentary flash of recognition from the occasional person on the street, even if it didn't mean much. I liked the idea that people were seeing me and thinking, "Where have I seen you before?" The next step, I thought, was for them to tie my name to my face and wonder, "Aren't you Jim McMullan?"

But that day was far ahead of me. I had to learn to walk before I could run.

Still, I was making good money doing episodic television. My agent was usually able to get me the standard fee called "top of the show," which was then $1200 for a week's work. Then if I was booked for multiple appearances or multiple weeks, the fee would be adjusted accordingly. The cherry on top, though, was when the show would cast me as a continuing character, someone who would appear regularly, as I had done in *Ben Casey*. So, you'd return to the set week after week and soon, those weekly paychecks piled up.

Of course, that was just wishful thinking, and the reality was much different. Rarely did a one episode character blossom into a multi-episode character.

"It can throw series planning on its ear," was the way one producer explained it to me.

"You're all set up for the season, each episode decided, casting done, scripts ready. And then a new face comes in. It's like making a three egg omelet, and when you're halfway done, someone throws in two more eggs. What's that going to do to the ingredients already in there?"

A few weeks after my *Ben Casey* work finished, I got a call from my agent. "You still good about doing episodic television?" he asked.

I'd told him about the unfriendliness and stress that had permeated the *Ben Casey* set.

"As long as Vince Edwards isn't involved," I said.

"You're not alone with that thinking, you know."

By this time I'd heard more stories about the nasty ways Edwards treated people on the set and about how he simply expected every woman who appeared on the show to belong to him.

"A piece of work, isn't he?" I asked.

The agent laughed. "Sometimes, they forget to leave the New York attitude behind when they come out here. He'll learn, eventually."

It wasn't long after this confirmation call that the agent rang me with some good news.

"You ready to try another television series?"

"No Vince Edwards, I hope."

"Who?" he responded innocently, then he laughed. "Consider that book closed, my friend." Then, he mentioned a popular series that had been running for a while. 'You ever hear of *Twelve O'clock High*?

The story dealt with the U.S. Air Force, and the title came from a World War II expression U.S. planes used to locate the enemy around them. The agent didn't wait for my answer. "I got you a nice part in the series," he said. "You'll be working with Robert Blake."

I'd never worked with him before, but I'd heard about him. He'd starred, as the murderous lead in *In Cold Blood*, the movie version of Truman Capote's best selling book of the same name, and the reviews had been excellent. I'd also heard he could be difficult to work with. "An angry guy" is the way a mutual friend described him, "troubled, kind of an outlaw attitude." But I never saw that side of Blake. He came to work on time, knew his lines and we interacted easily over the week we worked together. He played a Native American who was a self-confident, seat-of-the-pants pilot. I was also a pilot and the third lead was Roy Thinnes (*The Invaders*) with whom Blake's character had a serious conflict. Thinnes's pilot was everything Blake's pilot was not, frightened, flying "by the book," unimaginative. But in the end, Thinnes saves Blake's life and becomes an unlikely hero.

There's a funny thing about the television world. From the audience perspective, it must seem as if there are literally thousands of people knocking on the door seeking to become part of it, whether acting, directing, producing or working behind the camera. Even then, the 1960s and 1970s, there were numerous networks offering a wide variety of programming, from dawn into the late evening, every day, week after week, and opportunities could seem boundless. But the truth, as is so often the case when you explore another's unfamiliar existence, is much different.

The television world, even now, is smaller than most realize. If you've worked with someone once, and you've been around television for a few years, the chances are you'll work with that person again.

On *Twelve O'Clock High*, the director was Robert Douglas, and it was a pleasure to work with him. Douglas was experienced, and it showed. He respected the actors and he rarely substituted his own judgment for the way an actor would play his or her role. He was approachable, open to suggestions from actors and seemingly grateful for them. It didn't hurt, I suppose, that he had been an actor himself before he turned to directing, and that he had distinguished himself on both sides of the Atlantic in live theater. Born and raised in England, he carried a quiet civility, and by the time I met him in the mid 1960s, he had built an enviable career directing both in movies and on television.

By now, my freelance acting career was moving along well enough. My agent had secured me several additional roles on network television, and I was enjoying my bachelor life in Southern California. A few months after *Twelve O'Clock High*, the agent called with the news that he had found me a spot on another network show, *The FBI*. It starred Efrem Zimbalist Jr. as an FBI inspector and was based on actual files.

"When's the audition?" I asked, figuring I'd have to convince some casting people I'd handle the role.

"Relax," he said. "The role's yours."

It's a truism in the acting world: When you don't have to audition for a role, when it's *you* they really want, it's a major career step.

"No audition?"

The agent chuckled. "They liked the film I sent over from *Ben Casey* and it looks like you've got a friend in the casting office."

Then, he told me the show would be directed by Robert Douglas. "He was impressed by your work on that fly boy show you did a few months back. He wants you for this role."

It's a great feeling when you're handed something like this, with no audition. The director knows and likes your work. You can go in feeling confident. For that moment, you're special, and no one can take that away from you.

I played a wealthy character who drove a fancy sports car and got kidnapped. Martin Sheen and Ed Asner played the kidnappers, and this was the first time I had met or worked with either of them. The moment I walked on the set, Robert Douglas gave me a big smile and said how glad he was to be working with me again, as gracious as ever. I had a good feeling about the show. Sheen and Asner were sharp, pleasant and talented. They gave you a lot to work with and we developed a good sense of interplay. With some actors, that doesn't happen. They can say their lines but there's no connection between how they say it and what you are saying. (I think of Vince Edwards in this connection.) There's no interplay between you, and the aura of authenticity in the scene just fades away.

Not so with Sheen and Asner. Before every scene, one of them would say, "Let's go over our lines, get a feel for the characters." We'd work out whatever kinks there were. Years later, I had the opportunity to work with both of them again and they remained just as professional, just as committed to a strong performance as they had been.

After the last day of shooting, Marty Sheen asked me to do him a favor and drive him to a Mazda showroom in Santa Monica. Mazda had introduced a radically new rotary engine called the Wankel, and Marty was excited about owning a car with one. After picking up the car, he invited me for a beer back at his house in Malibu where I met his lovely wife Janet and his kids, Charlie, age three and Emilio, age six. Little did I know that those cute kids would go on to have successful careers of their own.

As I left Marty that day, I felt a special connection with him. In addition to acting with him years later, our paths crossed on more than one political protest march. In 2003, for example, a group of us, Marty included, marched down Hollywood Boulevard to protest the Iraq war, and my wife, Helene, as well as our two sons, Sky and Tysun, were also there carrying signs that demanded "NOT IN OUR NAME!"

When I think back to these early acting credits, I'm struck by two things: first, the seeming ease with which I slipped into the life of a professional freelance actor. I had had no serious training, other than the occasional role in a college production, yet each step along the way prepared me for the next, and I never had issues with career promotion or ambition to succeed. It was as if I simply glided along, confident and content, moving from one role to the next, assuming the future would take care of itself.

Second, I probably should have developed a more professional background for myself, taken acting classes, gone to advanced acting school, worked harder on being the best actor I could be. But I didn't do any of those things. I looked on acting as having fun. I was young and single, and the studios and networks were actually *paying* me to enjoy myself.

Sometimes I think back and wish I'd had the passion to do workshops and live theater during those early days. There is no question that it would have made me a better actor and perhaps more famous. But then, I think about what I would have given up: going to the beach for the entire day, late night bonfires with friends, motorcycle adventures and random, spur-of-the-moment trips to exotic places.

A hard-working, serious minded actor wouldn't have had time for all of that.

Actually, I did get fairly close to stardom. But the difference between me and the stars is the stars really, really worked hard, every day and rarely took a break. They were so dedicated.

But me? I guess you'd have to say I was content having a good time.

Chapter Five

A Starring Role...Finally

WHILE MY ACTING career was slowly building, my personal life was undergoing change. I never considered myself religious, aside from some early years spent as an altar boy at St. Ignatius Catholic Church in Long Beach. My mom was a devout Catholic and my dad was a devout atheist. So in the morning, I'd be filled with church doctrine and in the afternoon my dad would lecture me on the evils of organized religion.

Somehow, through that contradictory period, I acquired a feeling that there was "something" out there which controlled our destiny, something larger than ourselves that we should come to terms with. As I searched for answers, I found only confusion, and I felt my mind fill with dead ends and no clarity. I wanted answers but the more I searched, the more the answers eluded me.

Then, one day in 1966, my good friend and actor, Tim McIntire, introduced me to LSD, and that experience opened the door to a whole new view of what spirituality was all about and kicked off my search in earnest. First, it was Transcendental Meditation, then Hinduism, then Buddhism, then numerous other "isms" and seminars and spiritual workshops, including EST. I tried them all and gained insight with each experience. But I wanted some place to settle, where I could find tranquility and fulfillment, especially at a time when my career was developing.

Surprisingly, in 1968, I found a temporary home in the teachings of L. Ron Hubbard and his philosophy of Scientology. From the 1950s onward, when Hubbard began to proselytize, Scientology has been a third rail for orthodox religious believers. Many dubbed it a cult, a scam, an anti-religion, because it was so enveloped and controlled by the personality and views of its founder. And I'm certainly not going to quarrel with that.

But for a young actor, single, on the cusp of stardom and floating free in the profane yet exciting world of television and movies, there was something alluring about finding answers to elusive spiritual questions. To me, it did not matter from where those answers emanated.

What I discovered was that Scientology, at least at first, offered me a lot of spiritual freedom, unlike the established religions with their ancient liturgies and their formalized worship processes. Scientology provided me the chance to clear my mind (to "get clear" in Scientology parlance) and wipe away the clutter that had accumulated through my ineffective and often frustrated searching elsewhere.

And it made me a better actor, too. I was more disciplined because my mind was clearer.

For a brief period, my world seemed balanced and tilted toward the stars. About a year after I got involved with Scientology, Tangie Miles, a friend who worked at Liberty Records, invited me to a party. I had been spending a lot of time with the people I had met through Scientology and she wasn't sure that was such a good thing.

"You're only hearing one single point of view," she said, "and there are a lot of people who don't agree with what these Scientologists say and think."

My answer was a smile and a reassuring nod. "It's not like I'm being brainwashed. How does it hurt to just listen?"

Of course, my involvement was deeper than that, but I wasn't someone who sought confrontation, and I remembered what I'd learned when young: Two things you never argue about are politics and religion.

"Anyway," I added, "I'm an actor. *That's* what my life is about."

My words seemed to satisfy her and then she mentioned her party. "I'm having a few friends I haven't seen in a while." Her eyes twinkled mischievously. "And none of them are into Scientology."

It turned out I knew almost no one at the party. For some that could be a downer, but long ago I saw a roomful of strangers as an opportunity. Pick out someone who looks interesting, I told myself, someone dressed differently, someone wearing their hair differently, someone with arresting eyes or a unique quality to their voice. And you might learn things you couldn't imagine.

Over the years it had worked for me, and now, I figured I'd try it again. Standing by herself across the room was a slender, shapely blond woman. She held a drink, but it seemed more like a prop than an indulgence because the glass never touched her lips. She surveyed the dozen or so people around her, a quiet smile across her face and seemed at ease. I tried to remember if I'd seen her before.

Somehow, I found myself standing right next to her.

"I'm Jim," I said, realizing she had been watching me as I had approached.

The soft smile remained, and when she spoke, I could sense a performer. "Helene," she said, "a California transplant, I'm afraid."

"Me, too," I said, sensing a connection that remains unbroken to this day. We began talking, and soon we were making plans to see one another again. It turned out Helene was a singer and had been touring the world for two years with a pop rock group called The Two People. She had just finished performing in Los Angeles, and she'd gotten to know Tangie a couple of years earlier while recording at Liberty Records. She had no idea I was on television or in the movies because she rarely watched either of them.

In my vibrant and comfortable Hollywood world that was certainly different. And somehow it added allure. She was about to tour New Zealand and Australia in a Broadway-based musical so there was no point pushing anything.

But I did a bit of research to find out her tour schedule. I wrote her friendly letters and enjoyed equally charming responses. At that point, it was friendship, although deep down I sensed stronger feelings developing.

When Helene returned from tour, she made a major decision. She was going to pursue her singing career, but as a single. "My old partner and I just had growing artistic differences," she said. "I respect him and his talent, but it's time for me to be on my own."

"How do you feel about Scientology?" I threw out, figuring a change of pace couldn't hurt.

She gave me a puzzled look. "What's it about?"

After we'd spent less than an hour talking, I could see she was intrigued. And sure enough, the next morning she went down and signed up. Like me, she had been spiritually rootless for quite a while, searching for answers but not finding them in organized religions. Now, she felt that so many things might become clearer if she tried something different, something outside the usual religious path. I remember her reaction after we had spent her first hour at the Los Angeles Scientology Organization.

"Wow!" was the first thing she said.

Helene and I started seeing one another while getting more involved with Scientology.

We even helped start something called the Celebrity Center, where Scientology scheduled you for public appearances to promote the program, and because of your "celebrity" status, it's expected you to help convince others to join.

I was able to keep up with my acting work even as I developed a closer and closer relationship with Scientology and with Helene. By that point, I had changed agents a couple of times. Marvin Burt had decided to go into semi-retirement, and I knew I needed a younger, more active representative. But agents aren't like oranges or rubber tires. They don't look or act alike.

They have different areas of expertise, and you get along with some and you don't get along with others. After about a year in Scientology, I was just getting to know Saul, my latest agent, a sharp young man who had grown up in West Hollywood and had embraced the movie and television business as if his life depended on it. He was over the top with ambition, not only for himself, but for each of his clients, and that usually signaled success. One day, he called me.

"Today's your good day, my friend," he began, and then he told me about a new movie being cast which would highlight the current culture clash between the hippie generation and an older, staid middle class. "It's a natural, the kids against the over thirties, and..." He paused dramatically. "They want you for one of the leads. You!" he practically shouted.

The movie was called *The Baby Maker* and the story concerned a middle class wife who was unable to have children. The couple got involved with a promiscuous young flower child, and saw her as the answer to their baby problems. They decided to have the husband impregnate her, so that the couple could walk away with the baby.

"The best part?" Saul added. "It's being written and directed by James Bridges, and he's really, really hot right now!"

I had no idea who James Bridges was. In coming years, he would write and direct major films like as *The China Syndrome* and *The Paper Chase* and *Urban Cowboy*. But at that point, his credits were still building. According to Saul, he had the director's equivalent of the actor's "it," that special something which set you apart.

"It's a big role, a leading role," he went on. It was larger than anything I had done. I was to play opposite Barbara Hershey, a young actress the studio was especially high on. And the movie fit right into the dramatic cultural changes playing out across the country.

But I had a problem and it was called Scientology. For about a year, I had been growing more involved with work at the Scientology center and with the briefing course we had developed for celebrities. In addition, Helene and I were training to be auditors, and this was a very prestigious position in Scientology.

So, before I agreed to the movie, I figured I'd better check with the Center, and when I did, I got a major surprise.

"We don't think you should leave the course," I was told. "You are helping so many people. You are needed. You are helping to save the planet."

"But this could be a starring role," I argued. "I've waited a long time."

"Your work is more important here, far more important," was the reply.

After I thought it through and felt the closeness and the bonding that the Scientology experience had given me, I came to a reluctant, though painful conclusion.

I met with Saul and told him I would turn the role down. "I'm in the middle of a course--" I started to explain.

His eyes grew large and he popped to his feet. "A course? What do you mean, a course?"

He started shouting at me. "This is an amazing opportunity, to star in a role with this hot new director! You'd have to be crazy to turn it down! Crazy!"

"I'm doing what I think is right. Acting isn't something that consumes my life, you know."

He stopped shouting long enough to stare at me long and hard. "Well. It. Should!" He stormed off.

The next day, Bridges called me. I could tell he was having a difficult time keeping a calm tone. "I don't understand what's going on here. Something about Scientology, I'm told, but I want *you* for this movie, I need you in the part."

"It's nothing personal," I tried to reassure him. "I'd love to work with you but I have other obligations, and right now, that takes precedence."

I could hear him take a deep breath. "I saw you in *Dr. Kildare* and *Ben Casey*, I thought you were great, just right for the husband role in this movie. Same kind of character. Youngish, clean-cut, earnest, sensitive." He paused. "I *really* want you to do this part."

"I just can't," I said and feeling so righteous about it. Looking back, I can see I was thoroughly brainwashed by Scientology, I was convinced my choice to reject the part was best for me and for the world in which I would eventually serve. My actor's life was supposed to support a greater purpose through Scientology. It did not matter as much what a most skillful director thought.

"Sorry," I added, and we hung up.

Looking back, it was obviously a bad decision, but at the time both Helene and I were obsessed with Scientology and how it was going to help so many people. We saw it as the path to worldwide peace, a way of life which sought to transform our burdensome existence on this earth into something serene.

A year later, we had lost our fixation on Scientology and its promise of transformation.

We came to see the program as promoting a cult-like existence where maintaining power over the lives of others far surpassed actually making those lives better. Our self-questioning began to erode our interest in the program. At the same time, I saw how my decision to reject a leading role in *The Baby Maker* added a question mark to my availability for any future movie project.

Suppose McMullan signed a contract and then his Scientology friends said not to take it.

The result was a slowing of acting opportunities. Movie producers are no different than the people who do the hiring in other industries. They want control and they want certainty their decisions will be carried out. Word spreads quickly in Hollywood, and I sensed my clean-cut, good guy image among producers was losing steam after I turned down James Bridges. Helene and I had been seeing more and more of one another, and as that relationship heated up, my acting life was cooling off. It was frustrating, and for the first time since that fateful day beside William Inge's pool years before, I wondered about my future as an actor. The fact that Helene and I were pulling away from Scientology meant little to producers who knew my James Bridges story. They were a cynical group and figured that if it could happen once, it could happen again.

And there were lots of actors out there.

On a basic human nature level, I suppose I would have to agree with them. But then again, I knew myself, and while I make mistakes like anyone else, I do not repeat those mistakes. I learn from my errors.

About a year after I turned James Bridges down, I got a call from Saul. It had not been a productive year for us. He resented my refusing the role in *The Baby Maker* and he saw my acting opportunities dry up. In fact, when I first heard his voice on the phone, I expected him to announce he would no longer be representing me.

Instead, there was a welcome lilt to his tone. "Jim," he said, "I've got something here just for you." He mentioned the name Robert Redford and that got my attention. It seemed that Redford, whom I had never met, and a hot young director, Michael Ritchie, who had made a name for himself in television, were putting together a feature film on ski racing. "They're calling it *Downhill Racer* and Redford's gotten a million bucks from Paramount to go shoot the movie in Switzerland and Austria. This is going to be big, Jim." The planning was well underway. Redford had cast Gene Hackman as a ski coach, and he'd already made a special trip to eyeball a couple of the famous European ski races. "He took a small crew with him and did some actual shooting over there," Saul added.

Then he said, "And they want to talk to you."

Redford. Skiing. Europe. What's not to like about *that*?

Saul made a quick phone call and set up a meeting for the next day. And suddenly, the actor's life looked pretty damn good again.

The following afternoon I walked into Redford's office, not sure where all of this was headed, but sensing something good was going to result. Only two people were in the room, Redford and Michael Ritchie. Redford introduced himself, then Ritchie, and added he'd been looking forward to meeting me. What I didn't know until later was they had already looked at some of my film and had decided they didn't need to audition me. I guess what they saw from my clips was enough because Redford motioned for me to sit, and then he gave me his steady blue-eyed stare.

"You ever do any skiing?" he asked.

I told him I had, though I'd never tried any thing more than the intermediate slopes. "I'm no expert," I said.

He waved off my comment with a brief smile.

Then, Michael Ritchie said, "Let me tell you the story we're going to do." Redford was going to play the lead, a cocky, ambitious guy on the way up, and the role they had for me was an older skier, a nice guy and champion whom Redford's character was aiming to replace. The competition between the skiers would be the major drama in the movie, but there would also be sharp, personal interchanges too, and a steady level of excitement would permeate throughout.

After Ritchie finished going through the story line, Redford took a deep breath and said, "Okay, that's what it's about. Do you want the part?"

Everything stopped suddenly and there was a long silence. I'd never had anything happen to me like this: no script reading, no audition, no wading through competition from other actors.

"You mean, that's it?" I managed. "I don't have to read anything?"

Redford smiled and nodded. "If you want the part, you got it."

My character was based on Buddy Werner, a top U.S. ski racer who was extremely popular and a great ambassador for the sport. Redford's character was a young hotshot with an attitude. He was pushy and he lived for the time when he would become the world downhill champion. Both of our characters were members of the U.S. Olympic team, and I played the top racer on the team. But during a big race, I lost a ski, fell and got injured. Redford's character visited me in the hospital and he couldn't hide his mixed emotions. He had sympathy for my injuries but was elated that I wouldn't be around to beat him in the next race. In the end, Redford's character won his big race.

My working with Redford was one of the best experiences I ever had in the movies. We shot in Kitzbuhl, Austria, Wengen, Switzerland and Provo, Utah, a month or so at each location.

The camaraderie on the set, along with the low-key, improvisational style of Michael Ritchie's direction, made for an exciting, fulfilling time.

Ritchie himself had such a creative approach. One time, we'd finished shooting a scene and we were walking back to the hotel. He saw some young women standing across the street, waiting for a bus.

He said to me, "Go over there and get in a conversation with them. I'll film it from here, but don't look back at us." Later, he told me he would use the footage as background when building my character, even though it wasn't set up in the regular script.

When I had left to go on location with Redford, I was living in an apartment about a block away from Paramount studios. In fact, there had been a plaque outside the building that read, "Jack London lived here," along with the dates. I discovered London did some work at Paramount in those early years, and when he did, he lived in the same building. It gave me a good feeling to know the spirit of the great story teller, the writer of *The Call of the Wild* and *White Fang*, resonated throughout the site. A small part of me even hoped that one day, well into the future of course, I might be cast in a movie based on a Jack London story.

But sadly, that day never did come.

I did have Robert Redford, though, and for the moment that seemed enough. Shortly after my casting meeting with Redford and Ritchie, I got a call. We were heading for Europe and would be shooting most of *Downhill Racer* in Austria and Switzerland.

"Bring enough to wear for at least three months," I was told. "Don't leave any loose ends behind."

For me, a major concern was my apartment. I loved the location, so close to Paramount and in the heart of Hollywood. I'd be leaving it empty for three months and I still had the rent to pay.

Once again, fate intervened. My relationship with Helene had been growing stronger, and just days before I was to leave for Europe, she called me.

"I need a place to live," Helene said. "My roommate's getting married next week and wants our apartment."

She asked me if I knew of anything available. "I'd even share with someone I didn't know," she said. "I'm kind of desperate."

The old saying about opportunity knocking when you least expect it seemed appropriate, I guess, because here I was about to vacate my apartment for three months and Helene was in need of a place, at least temporarily.

"How about staying here," I suggested, "in my apartment?" Then I realized that sounded more intimate than I wanted it to. "I mean, I'll be away for the next three months. This place will be empty and, well, you could stay here."

She understood what I was offering, "That would be great," she said, and that's what we did. I left for Europe, Helene moved into the apartment, and we kept in touch by mail.

Everything fell together with the movie, too. It was a joy to be working with such dedicated people. For Redford, this was a chance to be a producer, the first for his Wildwood Productions. For Ritchie, it was his chance to move out of directing for television and into the feature film world. The energy and enthusiasm was magnetic and *Downhill Racer*, more than fifty years later, is now a classic ski film. I'm so proud to have been a part of it.

Three months later, I moved back in the apartment and Helene didn't move out. And just like that, we had become a couple.

Every actor harbors the dream that someday that people will refer to your name and "star" in the same breath. To be described that way is the pinnacle of success in our business. And I was no different from any other young actor. It was my ultimate goal.

And after *Downhill Racer*, I was on the verge. Working with Gene Hackman and Robert Redford, two established stars, having my movie credit line directly under theirs, playing a character who had significant influence on how the story developed all fed into my growing awareness that stardom was not just a fantasy for me.

Two months after returning from Europe and settling in with Helene at the apartment, one of the largest theatrical agencies in the world, International Creative Management (ICM), got in touch, and it came at a perfect time. Saul, my agent, had decided he'd had enough of the movie business and wanted to hang out in the Pacific Northwest, among the redwoods and the blue Norwegian pines, and I waved a grateful goodbye to him.

As if it had been scripted, ICM came along and got right down to business. "We've watched the *Downhill Racer* footage and we like what we've seen," one agent told me. "We want to represent you."

I was flattered, of course. ICM was a giant in the talent agency business, they represented many at the top of the movie profession. And when they came to you and not the other way around, it meant they had something important in mind.

And sure enough, within days after signing with them, they asked me to stop by the office for a conference. There were these "two kids" from Houston, Texas, they said. They had written a script and shopped it around Hollywood. The ICM veteran agents then shook their heads, more in wonder rather than disbelief. The "kids" had almost no movie experience. But, somehow they'd gotten financing, and also found a producer. They had seen my work in *Downhill Racer* and they wanted to work with me.

Then came the clincher. One of the ICM agents said, "We think you could be the star of this movie."

There it was, finally, the word "star."

The kids were David Frost and J.P. Feigelson, and when we met at the ICM offices, they both said enthusiastically, "We want you for this movie."

So I signed up, and was ready, for the first time to have top billing.

If I had been able to look into the future, toward the end of the movie, I don't think I'd have been doing happy handsprings.

The movie was called *The Windsplitter*, taken from the model name for an oversized and very popular Harley-Davidson motorcycle. Throughout this movie, I was the man on the Windsplitter. My character, Bobby Joe Brandon, came from a small Texas town, went off to Hollywood and became a movie star. The town invited him back to celebrate his success, a local boy who really made good. As the movie opened, my character rode into town on his big Harley, wearing scruffy clothes, leather fringe on his jacket, long hair, clearly not the image of conventional success the town fathers expected. Town officials expressed regret for inviting my character and they spent the remainder of the movie trying to get rid of him. Rumors spread that he was carrying all sorts of drugs: marijuana, cocaine, heroin.

They hired some bad guys to go after my character, to scare him off, but he hung in and didn't leave. Eventually, there was a showdown and after they killed his dog, Maggie, he concluded he had had enough and headed back to Hollywood.

We shot the movie in Columbus, Texas, a small town just south of Houston. As befitting a star, I had my own dressing room for the eight weeks we were there. But this was a super low-budget film. When they could, they used local people, buildings and street scenes. Even the town mayor had a role, and for extras, the producers rounded up student actors from the nearby universities.

I was so engrossed with making my role work that I overlooked how this low-budget attitude might affect the film, itself. I didn't realize it until later, but the script, written by the director, J.P. Feigelson, was stilted and lacked subtlety. I was so excited to be starring in a movie of my own that I overlooked the obvious flaws. J.D. was a very pleasant young man, as was the producer, David Frost, but the neither of them was experienced. J.D. had won an award for a short film, and this was his first shot at making a feature film. He didn't have that bursting sense of creativity an actor likes to see, and he wasn't able to "make magic" happen on the screen.

All of this never fully struck me until we were wrapping the film for post-production. I finally saw the movie in its entirety, and that's when the writing and directing flaws hit me. By then, of course, it was too late to do anything but vow that next time, I'd keep a better eye on how a film was evolving and on the script's authenticity. It saddened me, though, because I had really struggled to make my character real, yet the lines had just not been there, and the direction had been pedestrian, at best.

For better or worse, though, I had my first starring role, and even with the writing and directing problems, there were some compensations. The movie premiered in Houston, and the producers still had high hopes for it. A week's worth of parties were arranged. Lots of local and national press members were around. Helene and I were feted as if we were visiting royalty. The steady beat of attention during that week might convince anyone we were destined for success, and for a brief moment or two, I bought into the idea. After all, with the media lined up to interview me, my smiling photo greeted me wherever I went, it was difficult not to get caught up in the buzz.

But reality wasn't far away. It wasn't that moviegoers didn't like the film or found it offensive. "Boring" was the most common reaction. No one could feel transported by it. No one could find memorable lines to repeat or dramatic scenes to recall. In the familiar parlance of movie reviewers through the generations, the movie simply didn't "work."

But I had my first starring role and there was a future to look forward to.

And there was an added bonus. During the eight week shoot, I made friends with the editor of the local Columbus newspaper, and I told him I was about to propose to Helene. He allowed me to reprint the cover page of the paper with a photo of me and Helene and a caption that read, "JIM POPS THE QUESTION!!!"

I inserted where the marriage ceremony would take place, the date (Christmas Day, 1970) and where we would honeymoon (Wengen, Switzerland, where we shot part of *Downhill Racer*).

Then, I gave Helene 100 copies which she sent to friends and relatives. So, *Windsplitter* wasn't a total bust, by any means.

Image Section

Pierce Brosnan and Jim discussing "Actors as Artists" where Pierce's paintings were featured.

Jim with children Sky and Tysun and Lee Majors on the set of "The Six Million Dollar Man"

Jim with Robert Redford and the cast of "Downhill Racer"

Jim sailing on "Zephyr" at the Jersey shore.

Jim with Helene, Sky and Tysun on the set of "Beyond Westworld" 1980

JIM MCMULLAN

Jim 2013

Jim McMullan

Jim as Senator Dowling in "Dallas" 1985

Jim in "The Windsplitter" 1969

Early Hollywood days

Jim in "Stowaway to the Moon" wearing Rusty Schweickart's space suit, borrowed from NASA, 1975

Image Section • 85

Jim in Ready Bank of San Antonio, Texas television commercial

Jim with Connie Selleca in "Beyond Westworld" 1980

Jim with Earl Holliman in the made-for-tv movie, "The Desperate Mission"

Jim with Charles Bronson on the set of "The Assassination" 1987.

Jim as Buffalo Bill

Jim in his New Jersey studio with published copy of "Actors as Artists"

Jim and Helene at Christmastime celebrating their anniversary

Chapter Six
Bread and Butter

MOST ACTORS, IF they've been around a while, understand that a career in television or movies needs more than the occasional starring role or special performance. While these can spot-light an actor's career high points, they aren't enough to fill in the days and weeks when the actor isn't working. They aren't sufficient when the rent comes due, the car needs transmission work or a son's college bill must be paid. It's a well-worn adage that "bread and butter" jobs pay the actor's day-to-day expenses as he or she travels from one rung in the career ladder to the next.

Bread and butter: The not-so-glamorous, not-so-attention-getting, not-so-well-paid roles that provide regular work so the actor can meet those bills and feel the satisfaction any contributing member of society would feel. For an actor, bread and butter comes with episodic television, and for me, it meant the 1960s, 70s and 80s episodes of weekly television shows.

There would be one or two regulars on a show but other actors would appear, often just for that one show, and sometimes they would have guest star billing, as I often received. Other times, you'd have to swallow a less prestigious role and a smaller check, but the key was you were continuing to work and that meant those threatening bills could be paid.

One of the more popular shows on episodic television was *The Rockford Files* which starred James Garner as a private detective who lived casually and unceremoniously on the beach in Southern California. What I liked about working on this show was Garner himself, and the way he ran things. He treated us all like family, even if you were there for a single episode. He kept things loose and comfortable.

I remember my first day on the set. I walked in, Garner spotted me and came over, holding out his hand, and introduced himself. Then, he took me by the arm and we made the round of the cast members. To each person, he would say, "This is Jim McMullan. He's going to play Barry Brauder and I know he'll be great." It made you feel wanted and respected, and as it turned out, working with Jim Garner was one of the best acting gigs I ever had.

He even helped bust some role stereotyping I had fallen into. Most of the parts I got were as a nice character, honest, reliable, one of the episode's "good" guys. Rarely, did I play a villain or someone with bad things on his mind. I looked honest and that, generally, was the way my character was portrayed. But on one of my first *The Rockford Files* shows, Jim Garner and the producers decided to change that.

"Jim," Garner said to me one day, "how would you like to play a heavy for a change?"

They showed me the script in which my character, a petty criminal, was high on cocaine and trying to pay attention to Garner, who sought to get him out of prison so Garner could help nail a couple of really bad guys. My character did get out of prison but before he could do much, he was captured by the bad guys and salted away in a mental institution. Garner's character, Jim Rockford, located me and broke into the institution to rescue me. When he found me, I was lying on a couch, high on Quaaludes, passive and pretty much out of it.

But this was one time I wasn't really acting naturally. The day before we shot the scene, one of the other actors suggested I try a half of a Quaalude tablet to "see what it feels like." I figured, in my typical way, why not? It blew me away! So when we shot the scene the next day and Jim Rockford caught up with me in the institution, I played the role knowing exactly what my character would feel like: fuzzy. I figured out how he would respond, namely thick-tongued 78 and vague. It was one of the few times in my career I can honestly say I performed as a method actor.

One of the most enjoyable things about working with Jim Garner on *The Rockford Files* was how relaxed things were on set and how open Garner and the director were to suggestions.

My best experiences were with directors who would say, "Don't worry about getting the lines perfect. Make the character come alive." There's a freedom that comes when the director tells you that. But it's the opposite when the director says, "Don't screw up these lines. The writing is very important. You must get every line right." This rigid attitude creates a big problem for the actor, as there's a possibility it will make you tense.

Sometimes, though, the actor has to maneuver the director in such a way that the director is able to "see" the symbiosis between the actor and the role he or she covets. In the early 1990s, MGM was putting together a movie called *The Net*, and it starred Sandra Bullock and was directed by Irwin Winkler. By this time, 30 years or so after my amateurish screen test days, I had learned a thing or two about the business and how to think creatively and get a role. A friend had shown me the script, and from a single reading, I saw a part in there that I coveted. But the only connection I had to the production was a modest acquaintance with Mindy Martin, the casting director. I did not know the production people at MGM and I had never met the director. So, I felt a bit like a little boy at the circus, dying to get inside the tent, but unable to pay the admission.

And that's when some creative thinking took over. I decided to produce a self-made video. It meant reproducing and taping a similar scene to that called for in the script, where the character I wanted to play does his thing. The script set this up to be a beach scene and involved my character moseying along the water's edge, ruminating aloud to himself. I dressed the way I thought the character would dress, I learned the scene lines from the script, and I convinced my twenty-year-old son to use his video camera to tape the scene.

Once I had the finished product, I called the casting director, described what I had done and urged her to show it to the director.

"I didn't realize you worked on spec," she said.

"If it's the right role…" I started to say, but she interrupted. "You know we've cast someone already for this role?"

I didn't know, of course. "Oh, well." My heart sank a bit and I was about to kick myself for not checking ahead of time, when she added, "We haven't finished casting yet, so let me show this to the director, anyway."

A couple of days later, she called me back. "Bingo, Jim! Irwin Winkler loves your scene, and he wants to meet you. How's tomorrow?" By this point, the production was coming together very rapidly, and the meeting with Winkler would happen the day before they started shooting.

"What about the shooting schedule?" I asked, sensing Winkler's attention would certainly be on having everything ready to go on set, and I could be an afterthought.

"He wants to meet," she answered.

So, the next day, I went to the set, met Winkler and joined a group of actors sitting around a table. Everyone was holding a script and I realized I was the only one at the table who had not been cast in the movie. What am I doing here, I asked myself. I didn't get the part I had done the video for, so what was going on?

Winkler and the others began to read through the script aloud, and suddenly, midway, Winkler looked at me and said, "You could play this guy." It turned out to be a small part, an agitator at the airport. But in a flash, I had become part of the movie, and I was delighted. Apparently, Winkler knew he wanted me in his movie. He just didn't know where I'd fit. So, as we read through the script, he tried to visualize me in several different roles, and when we came to the airport agitator, it simply worked for him.

It was the strangest casting experience I ever had. But then, I had never done a "self- made video" before (or since).

Years before that strange experience with Irwin Winkler, I spent a lot of time making my way along the episodic television series trail, the bread and butter side of my career. It was the late 1960s, and my agent landed me a role on *Daniel Boone*, a popular weekly show that portrayed the life and times of the iconic frontiersman in the waning days of the 18th century. The show was set in Daniel Boone's hometown, Boonesborough, Kentucky, which, in those days was truly a rugged frontier town. Along with a regular cast of characters, each show included guest artists and an adventurous story from Daniel Boone's life. I ended up doing four of the shows and playing Mason Pruitt, a sometime side-kick of Boone's. Fess Parker was the star, and he was likable and very pleasant, not an ounce of self-importance in him.

He said to me one day, "I don't consider myself a great actor. I just show up and do my thing." When he said that, it reminded me of Spencer Tracy and Slim Pickens. I was working with a series of actors who relied on instinct.

My character always wore a big leather jacket, and somehow the producers discovered I could play the guitar and sing, although I had avoided all of that ever since I left college. So, in every show, they had me play and sing, and to be truthful, it was pretty corny. Imagine: I walked into a saloon where rough-edged characters played cards, downed shots at the bar, laughed up-roariously at one another's off-color jokes. Then, I pulled out my guitar, began strumming chords 81 and launched into a ballad which had absolutely nothing to do with the week's story line or the lives of the characters around the set.

I asked one of the producers, "Isn't this kind of phony or unrealistic?"

The producer laughed. "Come on," he said, "audiences love the romantic touch. Take a look at how musicals play on Broadway. No show's so serious you can't break in with a song."

Despite that, working on this show was like working on *The Rockford Files* some years later. I was part of a family, and for the first time in my career, I walked on a set in the morning and knew everyone. It made things very comfortable, and that was always an important thing for me. Usually, things don't work out that way on episodic television. In fact it's often the opposite.

You come in and no one knows who you are. You introduce yourself, maybe get a quick nod and a cold handshake from the producer and the star, and then, just as you're settling down, someone shouts, "Okay, let's get to it!"

If you had long or complicated lines in the opening scene, you did not benefit from previous work with cast or crew. No one clued you in to *how* the director wants them said. It would be natural to feel nervous, knowing you had to prove yourself, show why they hired you in the first place.

Most of the time I survived the challenge, but not always. A couple of times, though never on *Daniel Boone*, I forgot a line or two or and some stage business. I felt, even without seeing him, the director get angry. I had to shrug that off and concentrate on not screwing up the entire show. It made for a long day of shooting.

Then, there's also the script supervisor to deal with. He or she is there to make sure the dialogue and action conform to the script exactly. Imagine if the writer is also the producer. Do you think you could change a line, even a single word without express approval?

The script supervisor is like a script "guard" I suppose, and if he or she catches you missing or changing a line, you'll hear about it right away. It is easy to see how an actor can feel intimidated and think, Oh Christ, they're watching every freaking syllable! It doesn't take a genius to see what this would do to the actor's sense of self confidence and potentially to the production itself. My best acting, my best scenes were when I didn't have to deal with the script "guards," when I was allowed to put my own spin on a line or two, and hear, "Okay, you didn't get that exactly right, but no problem. Let's see how it plays when we rerun the tape."

And numerous times, the version with the slightly changed writing became the final version.

Around this time, in early 1970s, I found myself in a crisis of confidence with respect to my career. I had been hanging around with Jimmy Caan, and he had decided his future did not lie with television.

"I'm going to stick with movies, Jim," he said. "You should consider it." But I had my episodic television gigs, and they were paying the rent nicely. Knowing I had a place to work most weeks was calming and reassuring. Yet, I could also see Jimmy Caan making a go of it with his decision. He'd met Francis Ford Coppola and was beginning to get cast in Coppola's movies. What should I do, I kept asking myself, television or movies?

Back and forth I went, and my indecision actually affected my overall career path. I was offered parts which I turned down for reasons which now seem poorly thought out. For example, I turned down the part of Ray Krebs, a regular character on *Dallas*, when that show was just starting out because I didn't like the script. I saw it as episodic television, little more than a soap opera, even though it became a smash hit for years and years. But I was leaning toward doing movies, and *Dallas* didn't fit my planned path Any actor will tell you that ironies abound in this business, probably because so much of acting is based on emotional expression and planning for the future is often impossible. Who would have expected that ten years later, I'd appear on *Dallas* in a role some say I was made for.

At the time, Helene and I weren't married, and she couldn't understand my overall attitude about turning down roles.

"You shouldn't be so picky," she would say. "You're young with a great future ahead. Take a chance. You never know." She was more right than she realized. I turned down the part of B.J. Honeycutt (memorialized by Mike Farrell) on *M*A*S*H*, again because I didn't like the script. And here's the greatest miscalculation of all: I didn't think the show was going to make it.

I remember Helene's words with anguish, when I said no to *M*A*S*H*.

"At least go out and read for the part," she implored me.

Nope, I figured I knew better. There was Jimmy Caan doing his movies and succeeding, and I figured if I just remained patient, maybe the same thing would happen to me. So episodic television, my bread and butter, was going to sit on the shelf while I toyed with the notion that a movie career would beckon.

In the meantime, my agents were growing frustrated because I wasn't showing much interest in the episodic TV readings they had set up. One day, I had a call from Leo, the lead agent.

"Jimbo," he said, the name he always called me, "we got a problem."

I had a hunch what was coming.

"We had a call from Burbank. They say you never showed for the reading on that family drama they're putting together."

"It's episodic television, Leo. I'm having trouble getting excited about--"

"Look," he interrupted, "it's CBS, the Tiffany Network, you know? They've already reached out to someone else."

I wanted to tell him I was sorry, but before I could get the words out, he said, "We're done, Jimbo, finished. We can't represent someone who doesn't follow through on what we set up. A formal breakup letter will be coming."

And that was it. I had been fired by my agent.

I hadn't walked away from episodic television completely, however. If something interested me, really interested me, well, I was all in. That happened when I was contacted for a role in the popular show *Bracken's World* which was in its second season. It was an hour long drama, about a fictional movie studio, Century Studios, and the drama that played out there within its walls. Each week there was a guest star, and the list of those who had appeared was impressive: Anne Baxter, Lee Majors, Ricardo Montalban, Sally Field, Edward G. Robinson, Raquel Welch and so on. So, when I was offered one of those guest star roles, it wasn't to be some nameless sidekick or one of the bad guys. I would be the lead on that week's show, and the set, a large movie studio, felt familiar and comforting.

My character was an arrogant avant-garde music composer from New York, brought out to California to write music for movies and television. His arrogance stemmed from the fact that Los Angeles was not New York. He felt that what they produced in Hollywood, music as well as drama, was for the masses, not for people with taste and class. My character made clear that working in Hollywood, composing the music *they* wanted, was almost but not quite beneath him.

I thought it would make for an exciting, conflict-laden drama. And the producers decided I better look and sound like a composer, if I was going to play one. So they hired someone named John Williams to help me make it seem real. I had no idea who John Williams was. I assumed he was some hack studio musician who worked with actors as a separate gig and some limited role on a lesser known show. Instead, I found out he was a graduate of the Juilliard School in New York, had composed music for various television programs in the 1960s and had written the score for several movies, including *Valley of the Dolls* for which he had received an Oscar nomination. And all this was done before he was 40.

"John's waiting for you at the studio," a producer said. "Good luck." A few moments later, I walked in and there was a full orchestra setting up with a tall, angular guy off by himself.

"You must be Jim McMullan," he said, holding out his hand, smiling. "You ready to become a composer?"

I looked around the space, and it reminded me of the scoring stage I used to visit when I worked at Universal and had free roam of the premises. There were the musicians and up above them, a film clip was ready to run on a screen. The musicians weren't looking at it but the orchestra leader/composer was. This was the process of integrating the musicians playing with the film clip, in order for the running film clip to mesh with the recorded music.

"Let me show you how this works," John Williams said.

I told him about my experiences at Universal, and he smiled. "We've come a long way since then, you know." So he called a break and we sat off to the side, and I learned how to act like a music composer. "Here's the way you hold the baton," he said, "like it's a soft bird, looking for a rest between flights."

He had me practice waving the baton so much it seemed attached to my hand.

"Now, any composer has to know how to deal with musicians," Williams said, "and there's no school to go to for that." He advised me to treat them as I would other actors, with respect and patience, recognizing that just as with any group of actors, there could be the occasional musician who had a bad day.

"No way to foresee any of that," he added. "You or your character will just have to cope."

He was such a nice man, patient and enlightening. By the time I left the studio, I had as clear a handle on my role as any time in my career. I may not have been able to actually conduct an orchestra, but I sure felt as if I could play the part of an orchestra leader.

Sometimes, bread and butter jobs meant taking the actor's art to where the payoff was more spiritual than economic. The Catholic Church had been involved with television production for many years, using the medium to present its message in both live as well as taped formats. In fact, you can trace that church's involvement back to the 1940s and 1950s when Bishop Fulton J.

Sheen, a spellbinding speaker and highly respected theologian, had a regular live program that was watched by millions across the country. By the time I reached Hollywood in the early 1960s, many religions had embraced the television medium in both the performing as well as the production sense. Shows would broadcast religious observances, and the church would also produce programming that presented its message in a more subtle, more indirect way.

My involvement with the Catholic church fell into the second category. There was a show, *Insight*, produced each week in Los Angeles, which portrayed an original work of fiction but which followed an uplifting theme and presented a moral lesson. The show was produced by Father Bud Kaiser, a Catholic priest, well-experienced in television production and determined to bring his message to as many people as he could. The shows themselves were simple productions, with austere sets. The characters did not move around much. The emphasis was on dialogue.

What gave the show its unique character was that Father Kaiser filled the cast each week with as many well-known Hollywood names as he could convince to participate. This served two purposes: It guaranteed a sizable television audience because Father Kaiser shamelessly promoted the guest stars each week; and it provided Father Kaiser with a golden reputation among the Hollywood elite because he made it possible for film personalities to show their generous and compassionate sides by appearing on the shows. In many ways, it was a win-win for the Catholic church, for the guest stars and for Father Kaiser, as well.

I remember our conversation when he asked me to be on one of the shows. "You'll be paid, of course," he said. "It's not a lot, but all of us recognize you and the other actors are professionals, and you're giving us your precious time."

I thanked him, and he nodded, squeezed my upper arm and moved off.

A few days later, after I had performed, I received a check for $157 with the notation, "acting fee." Well, I thought, doing this show wouldn't make me rich, but the cause was good, and it made me feel good to do it.

The next day, I was on the set, watching a rehearsal for an upcoming show. The assistant director spotted me and came over. "Got your check, right?"

I nodded. "Thank you."

"The thing is..." he began, "I mean, you don't keep that money. No one does. You give it back."

There was a pause, and I must have looked very confused because he followed up with, "Father's doing a good thing here. Everybody *knows* that. Getting this show ready is expensive."

I must have looked resigned because the assistant director gave me a grin and said, "Father will take care of you. Don't worry."

So I gave my check back, and sure enough, several months later, just before Christmas, in the mail came a beautiful, hand-crafted wooden necklace made in Africa, a one-of-a-kind design.

Inside the box was a simple card that read, "Thank You, Father Bud Kaiser."

Chapter Seven

The Bionic Connection

By 1975, I had established myself in the television and movie worlds as a reliable actor who played youngish, good guy roles, a second or third lead who had an impact on the evolving story. My episodic television roles, coming as regularly as they did, provided a solid acting foundation, and I felt good about what I was doing and what the future could hold.

Was I working towards that elusive star billing that, so many years before, Jere Henshaw and Monique James at Universal had tempted me with when they saw my initial screen test?

Like many actors, the dream of becoming more well known fuels the reality of working hard each day, shrugging off inevitable disappointments and pushing on. The reality we live makes the dream seem remote, at times. But for many creative people, the dream never completely dies, and it was that way with me.

One evening in 1975, Helene and I went to a Hollywood party given by some actor friends. We had been married for five years, had two beautiful boys, Sky and Tysun, and had settled into a social world with other television/movie couples. There were, perhaps, twenty people at the party but the house was large and people were conveniently spread about. I was sitting on a couch with an open spot next to me; I looked up and for an instant, the world stopped spinning.

Directly across the room stood one of the most gorgeous females I had ever seen. Tall and curvy, in a tight dress with cascades of shining blond hair and a smile that lit up her face, she was speaking with a well-built, handsome man. It was obvious they were a couple. I recognized was Lee Majors, who had created *The Six Million Dollar* man character on television and had become known as "the bionic man." The series would be a major hit, no pun intended, with a spin-off series, films, books and comics. But I'd never seen her before. I turned to one of the hosts who had just taken my drink order:

"Who is *that*?" I asked, nodding towards the couple.

He chuckled. "Him or her?"

"Her," I said.

"She's Farrah Fawcett, and he's Lee Majors. Nice couple."

They had that look actors recognize in one of their own, a presence, even when the actor is simply relaxing.

"She's gorgeous," I said.

"Yup," the host grinned. He squeezed my shoulder and walked off.

About 15 minutes later, Lee Majors walked up, pointed to the empty spot next to me.

"Taken?" he asked.

"All yours," I said and scrunched over so he could sit comfortably. In front of us was a coffee table with a bowl of fresh fruit. In addition to several bananas and apples, it also contained a thick bunch of delicious looking grapes. And suddenly, I had an urge for grapes. They had a plum-like tint, and I could imagine the sweetness, the juiciness of them.

As I reached to break off a couple, I fell into a familiar habit that stretched back to my teens, completely unaware for the moment of where I was and who I was with. I broke off the first grape, flipped it into the air and caught it in my open mouth. Without missing a beat, I did the same with the second grape, and as I began chewing and enjoying the taste and texture, I realized that the guy sitting next to me, Lee Majors, was staring at me with a look somewhere between amusement and shock.

So I smiled at him, continued chewing my grapes, and held out my hand. "I'm Jim," I said.

He grasped my hand firmly. "How'd you learn to do that?" he responded.

I told him it was something we did in high school. "Some kids played cards, others pitched pennies. We used to throw grapes to one another," I said. "You learn to position yourself so you're as far under the grape's trajectory as possible. The secret is to have the grape drop into your mouth instead of trying to dig it out of the air."

"Let me see you do it again," the Six Million Dollar Man said. So I reached for another grape, popped it into the air and caught it with my open mouth.

"I could do that," he said.

I shrugged because, of course, anyone with a taste for grapes, a modicum of coordination and a welcoming, open mouth could do it when the grape was flipped from two-three feet away..

But the real test came when the distance between the flip point and your mouth stretched to five feet, ten feet and even farther. Then, catching the grape was a much bigger accomplishment.

"Yeah, I could do that," Lee Majors repeated.

"It can be harder than it looks," I said.

He pondered that for a moment. "What about you and I have a little competition. We'll flip grapes to each other and see who can catch the most?"

I figured what the hell. Helene was enjoying herself in the other room. She'd probably have tried to talk me out of what Majors suggested because of its high school overtones. And the bottom line was it was just innocent fun.

"Sure," I said, standing up and grabbing the bunch of grapes.

"Let's do it outside, otherwise, we'll draw a crowd and somebody will complain we're toying with food when there are starving people in, wherever!"

He had a point, though a bunch of grapes didn't seem like much of a symbol to me. But Hollywood was replete with attention seekers and rumor mongers, and you didn't have to be there long to learn to keep your guard up, even in the most innocent situations.

We walked out the back door and found a nice, quiet spot behind the garage. It was still light out, with the sun muted by partial cloud cover and almost no wind.

"You throw to me, and then I'll throw to you," he said. We stood about five feet apart, and we agreed to make each throw launch the grape higher than the throw before. The first one to miss three would lose the competition.

"Here we go," I said and flipped the grape about two feet into the air. He positioned himself well and caught it easily. Then he threw one to me which I also caught without a hitch.

"Round two," he said, and a grin lit up his face, as he waited for my flip. This time I tossed it three feet in the air and he had no trouble catching it.

Back came the grin as he tossed me the next one.

"Uh-oh," he said, as I misjudged the arc and the grape bounced off my nose.

"That's one," he added.

Back and forth we went. It was four rounds and the grapes were tossed six, seven feet in the air. By round six, he had missed two grapes to my one, and the grin had disappeared. I saw the competitive side of Lee Majors.

"Ready?" I asked, and he nodded.

I tossed this grape about eight feet in the air and watched its trajectory against the beginnings of a twilight sky. As the grape reached the top of its arc, I could see Majors position himself under it, his mouth open, his senses alert/ But somehow, he misjudged, and the grape caught him on the chin and fell harmlessly to the grass.

"Damn," he said, then he looked over at me and held out his hand, smiling. "This is just game one," he said. "I have a feeling we'll be seeing each other again real soon."

Why not, I thought. "I look forward to it," I said.

"Come on, let's go back into the house. I'll introduce you to Farrah."

In the following months I recalled the grape throwing incident every now and then, but I was busy with my career, and it slowly faded from my mind.

About six months later, my agent called. "There's this new hot show," he said, "*The Bionic Woman*. They want you to read for an upcoming role."

I'd been following the industry trades, and the show had premiered earlier in the year with Lindsay Wagner as Jaime Sommers, the female equivalent to Lee Major's *Six Million Dollar Man*. Like Majors's character, she had been physically altered by science to possess superhuman strength and athleticism, and her mission was to find and neutralize the bad guys, wherever she found them. Almost from its first episode, *The Bionic Woman* found an enthusiastic and adoring audience, no doubt helped along by its similarity to the continuing adventures of Steve Austin, the Six Million Dollar Man.

The Bionic Woman, Lindsay Wagner, was someone I had never met. But the story line sounded interesting. I would play the captain of a submarine that had been attacked, and Lindsay Wagner would come to the rescue. It turned out Lindsay was delightful to work with, a great stage presence and just a lovely person. Once in a while, you come across an actor you really get in synch with, someone you feel an instant connection with, and Lindsay happened to be that person.

She'd seemingly come out of nowhere, although actually, she'd been a hard working actress for quite a while, including a stint as a contract player for Universal, just like me. She landed the role of Jaime Sommers on an episode of *The Six Million Dollar Man*. Within a year, plans were underway to create her own show as a spin-off.

As I went through the script the night before the first day of shooting, I noticed that Lee was scheduled to be in the scene with Lindsay and me. And the first thing that came to mind was *grapes*. So on my way to the set that first day, I bought a bunch of grapes.

I settled in a chair off camera, placed my bag of grapes at my feet and was nibbling away when I sensed someone walk up behind me. Before I could turn, I heard, "You spare a few of those grapes, my friend?"

There was Lee, smiling and holding out his hand.

Then, he picked up a script and thumbed through the first few pages and handed it to me.

"Here I am," he said, and showed me the scene he was in.

He laughed. "Just a cameo, really, but the exposure never hurts, right?"

I could certainly agree with that.

"So." He pointed at the grapes. "You still popping those in your mouth?"

For an answer, I flipped one into the air and caught it between my teeth.

"Okay," he nodded, running his eyes over the set. "What about, see, over there, those big scrims?" He pointed at two flimsy extra large curtains, hanging together along the back wall of the set. Behind them, there seemed to be some empty space.

"It'll be an hour before they get their production wheels going. How about another grape throw, just you and me? They sure as hell won't miss us."

He was right about that. The production people, director and stage managers, script supervisor and property custodians were in small groups around the set. Scripts were passed back and forth. Some people pointed, others measured, still others wrote notes. It didn't look as if we were on the edge of rehearsing anything.

"Let's do it," I said, picked up my bunch of grapes and headed for the empty curtained area Majors had pointed out.

"Same rules?" I asked. "Three drops and you're out?"

He nodded and we positioned ourselves behind the curtains about three feet apart. I offered him the grapes. He snapped one off and lobbed it at me about a foot in the air. I caught it in my mouth and sent one back at him about the same height which he also caught.

We went back and forth, two, three, four feet apart. I hadn't missed one, but Lee wasn't having a good day. By the sixth throw, he'd already had a grape hit his chin and another catch him in the eye. Then, with seventh throw, now about eight feet high, he made a valiant effort but it wasn't meant to be, and the grape bounced harmlessly off his nose, falling to the ground.

"You're the champ," he said, holding out his hand.

"Call it my misspent youth," I answered, offering him the grapes to eat for real.

He snapped off a couple and put them in his mouth. "Eating grapes will have new meaning for me from here on, I guess."

After spending some more time with him, I got the feeling that Majors didn't consider himself a great actor, though he had a vital personality, was quite popular and had that look I've mentioned before. He was certainly capable. He worked hard, always knew his lines and was very professional on the set.

But I wondered about the range of his talent, his ability to play different characters with emotional peaks and valleys. As it turned out, he never did develop much of a movie career. He continued working in television for years, where he'd developed a big following.

About a month after we wrapped *The Bionic Woman*, my agent called and said Charles Fries Productions was putting together a two-hour television movie on Francis Gary Powers, the U-2 spy plane pilot who had been shot down over the Soviet Union in the waning days of the Eisenhower administration and held captive into the opening months of the Kennedy administration. It would be the story of how Powers was eventually freed through the diplomatic efforts of the major players in John F. Kennedy's cabinet.

"Lee Majors is going to play Powers," my agent said, "and they want you to read for the Bobby Kennedy part."

Read? I'd gotten used to being called and told I would be playing so-and-so. "You're sure?"

"Delbert Mann is directing, and this is what he wants," my agent said. I knew Mann by reputation. He'd won an Oscar for Paddy Chayevsky's *Marty*. I realized an actor could go through an entire career and never get the chance to work with someone like Mann. As it turned out, the reading went well, and Mann told me I had the part before I left the studio.

I knew I'd have to prepare very hard for the role. I'd never done Bobby Kennedy's voice, but I knew he had a pronounced Harvard accent, and he tended to talk in a staccato style. I wanted to sound as much like him as I could, but, of course, Bobby Kennedy wasn't around. His assassination in 1968 changed US history, as he likely would have been elected the next president.

I remembered a best-selling album from the Kennedy years. It was actually a spoof on the Kennedys, including their style of speaking, their accents and their way of life. Called *The First Family*, it was produced by comedian and impersonator Vaughan Meader, and it portrayed the Kennedy family members, particularly Bobby and Jack Kennedy. It had been an immediate success in 1962, selling over one million copies in a matter of weeks.

More than a decade later, I found the album. I must have played it 100 times in order to get familiar with his voice, the elongated *ahhhs*, the quick, sharp responses, the blunted consonants. Eventually, I felt I'd achieved the proper sound.

Later, though, listening to rehearsal tapes, I had the feeling it sounded a little like a caricature. But Delbert Mann and his production people had no problem with it, and they, of course, were my jury.

Lee Majors and I wanted to continue our grape competition, though it was tough for him to sneak in free time since he had the starring role in the production. But one day, he showed up on set with a bunch of grapes, and I knew we were on. He motioned me to walk outside the studio, and when we did, we were met by his driver (one of the perks for being a star) who took the grapes and moved to a permanent ladder that ran up the outside of the building to the roof.

"How about we change things a bit?" Majors asked. He suggested the driver stand on a ladder step and drop the grapes to us below. "Each round, he moves up one step."

Why not, I thought? It seemed fairer than each of us trying to copy the other's throw. And this way, there was only dropping rather than throwing involved.

The driver climbed to the third ladder step, turned around and waited with the grapes.

"Same rules?" Majors asked.

I nodded. "Three drops and you're out."

He walked over to the ladder, positioned himself under the driver's outstretched arm.

"Okay," he said.

In an instant the grape disappeared into his mouth. He moved aside so I could get position, and I nodded to the driver.

Round one, no misses. I caught the grape easily, but when the grape hit the back of my throat, it felt different than when I had caught one of Lee's throws. It was not as soft, as gentle, and it occurred to me that dropping a grape from a height could build greater momentum than a person could stand.

By the fourth round, I was convinced. When the grape slammed into the back of my throat, it hurt for an instant. I had caught every grape, but Majors had missed one, and now he readied himself for round five. The driver was standing on the eighth ladder step, which put him more than twenty feet above us.

"Do it," Majors said, and the grape was released from the driver's outstretched hand. It descended as if shot from a gun, and in an instant it reached Majors, only to miss his mouth and catch him in the eye.

"Ow," Majors grunted, as the grape bounced to the ground. He shook his head. "That sucker hurt," he said, rubbing his eye.

I knew where he was coming from, and it didn't figure to get easier the higher the driver climbed. "How about a truce?" I suggested. "No winner, no loser. And we polish off the grapes for lunch."

He thought about that for a moment, then he shrugged. "Sure beats ending up with a black eye, doesn't it?"

About a year later, Lindsay Wagner came back into my life, and I was delighted to work with her again. I played her love interest in an episode called "The Martians Are Coming." My part was Casey, an intrepid reporter, who was dispatched by his newspaper to quietly investigate this Bionic Woman and discover how she did her miraculous feats and where she got her strength. As it turned out, for the entire show I trailed after her, watching her jump up onto a tall cliff or speed down the road faster than the traffic. Casey saw her but refused to accept the fact that he was following a superwoman. He figured there must be a rational explanation and finally he confronted her, demanding to know how she pulled off such amazing physical actions.

But the Bionic Woman wasn't about to explain herself to a curious reporter who probably wouldn't understand anyway. She could have told him it was all a mirage or that she drank a magic potion each day.

But she handled it a different way. When Casey asked the Bionic Woman how she achieved her physical prowess, she gave him a measured look and said, "Don't bother me."

And with a sparkle in her bionic eye, she walked away and out of his life.

Lindsay had a successful run with *The Bionic Woman*, lasting three television seasons and developing a devoted national fan base. Working with her created chemistry that I never felt with an actress. She was always so professional, yet there was a warmth between us, a feeling of being in sync from the first day that we worked together. It made the acting flow so easily.

Several years later, I had the chance to perform with Lindsay again, though not on *The Bionic Woman*. That time, I played her husband in a made-for-television movie, *The Taking of Flight 847*, about the real-life heroics of a flight attendant during the vicious hijacking of a TWA plane bound for Rome from Athens. Lindsay played Uli Derickson, the German-born flight attendant who, because of her language skills, was able to communicate with the hijackers and keep the situation under relative control. In the end, the plane landed in Beirut, Lebanon and after 17 days on the ground, she was able to convince the hijackers to release the hostages, all but one of whom survived.

I enjoyed working with Lindsay again, and I did gain one small perk that never came up before. The script called for us to kiss. It was a time when AIDS was gaining a lot of attention, and people in the arts, especially theater, TV and film, were being watched with suspicion because so many were succumbing. It was a time before serious research had been done, and numerous theories about its causes were floating about, but few solid answers were available. Did you get it from sex, and if so, from only gay sex? Did you get it from what you inhaled? From what you swallowed? From what you touched?

No one really knew, yet we couldn't let it stop our lives. We couldn't call a halt to the intimacy, physical and emotional, that bonded people. People urged others to use protection, check your partner's sexual history, avoid promiscuity, limit your intimate moments to those you knew and trusted.

It was against this background that Lindsay and I faced that kiss the script called for. As we readied to rehearse the scene, she gave me a serious look, and in a hesitant voice she asked,

"You don't have AIDS do you?"

"No, I said, smiling, "no, I don't"

"Oh, good!" she laughed.

And when we had our script kiss, I thoroughly enjoyed it.

We never worked together again, but Helene and I bought a house in Pacific Palisades, and I learned that Lindsay also lived there. Occasionally, we'd run into one another and have a quick hello and a brief chat, but I did find out she had started a school for actors.

One day, she called me and asked, "Did you know there are numerous *Bionic* fan clubs across the country?" I didn't. She told me those fan clubs were obsessed with the show details.

Many had copies of the old scripts, knew all the characters and even staged recreations of the shows for their own pleasure. "They can describe who did what," she said, "and they know on which show each character appeared."

She told me all the Bionic clubs were coming for a major meeting, and they had offered to run a benefit for her acting school at a major Beverly Hills hotel. As part of the appeal, they wanted some of the Bionic Woman characters who had appeared on the show to be there. "I'd love for you to be one of them," she said. "It will really be fun."

This was a most pleasing idea. First, my memories of working on the show had been all positive. And secondly, because actors yearn for a touch of immortality in the roles they portray, and here, decades later, I would be given a chance to celebrate a role that spanned the generations. Finally, it would give me a chance to be around Lindsay for awhile.

So I readily agreed, and on the appointed day, I joined hundreds of people in a large Beverly Hills conference room to celebrate the days of *The Bionic Woman*. Lindsay was at the microphone, and she motioned for me to stand beside her. "Tell everyone about your experiences with the shows," she said, handing me the microphone and stepping back. So I talked about the pleasures of working with Lindsay and the crew, about how interesting the scripts had been, how strong the direction had been and how proud we all were to work on a show with a female lead who became a touchstone for women's physical prowess.

Then, I solicited questions and comments, and for many people, the episode, "The Martians Are Coming," when I played the intrepid reporter, Casey, had particular allure. Some recited lines from memory, including words I said on camera. They wanted to know how we approached the parts, if we ever improvised dialogue or changed the script in the middle of a performance. Lindsay and I talked about working with one another, and some of the questions were about how we prepared and what kind of critique we gave one another afterwards.

It was an amazing experience. There was this unusual subject, the bionic world, about which I had known nothing. Yet, thousands of people from across the country felt a vital and enduring connection with the actors and with the show, itself. And remarkably, these people had found one another because they shared a belief this television show had something important to say to them.

I found that very assuring, and when I left that day, I remember I couldn't keep a smile from my face.

Chapter Eight

The World of the Television Pilot

ONE DAY IN the early 1990s, I was walking down Hollywood Boulevard when I spotted a nicely dressed young man standing in front of a Cinemax theater. He was handing out flyers that contained the words "Tonight!" "Free!" "We Need YOU!" The flyers mentioned a showing of the newest Robert Altman movie, The Player, about the dangerous competitiveness of working in film studios, and they were looking for a "test" audience. I had to admit I was tempted to join the eager throng beginning to form around the young man with the flyers. I well remembered how the test audience format had impacted my career, and how watching a show at a special screening, even if you weren't in the movie or television business, made you feel like a special guest.

It also reminded me of the test audience we encountered years before, when we had wrapped *Downhill Racer*. Robert Redford had been enthusiastic about the movie from the first day, and the feeling around the set had been equally excited. We felt we had the ingredients for a successful movie: a strong cast, headed by Redford and Gene Hackman, a solid story line based on a book about ski racing by Oakley Hall and breathtaking scenery as we shot both in Europe and the western United States.

Then, we met our test audience at the screening Redford had arranged. There were about a hundred of them, up and down the age spectrum, chosen at random. When it was over, less than two hours later, there was momentary silence. Then, the buzzing of comments raced through the crowd. I was too far away to hear anything specific, but somehow I sensed a problem. It was as if you'd walked into a room, everything went quiet, and you knew someone had just mentioned you in an unflattering way.

In a moment, Michael Ritchie, the director, appeared. He thanked the audience for coming and mentioned the blank cards and ballpoint pens which had been on each of their seats.

"This is where you get the chance to grade us," he said, adding with a laugh, "and I hope you'll be generous with your praise." He asked them, specifically, to touch on how authentic the characters seemed to be, whether any particular character stood out, and if so, how and why. He requested feedback on whether the story held their attention throughout, and if not, where it broke down. He invited comments on the scenery and background landscapes and whether they added excitement to the overall story. Finally, Ritchie asked them how they would grade this movie experience with A-plus being the highest grade.

"Be frank," he said, reminding them their comments would not be personally attributable in any way. "What you say will help us with the final product. We want to make this into the best movie we can make."

A couple of hours later, after the test audience had left, we sat around a table going through the comments. And it was painful because all of us, Redford included, had come away from the screening feeling good about what we had seen.

But not so this test audience. "The characters are wooden," one person wrote. "You feel nothing for them."

Another wrote, "The pace was spotty, much too slow, except when they're racing."

A third informed us, "You need more action. The ski races get over too quickly, and then nothing much happens." A demand for more drama and authentic dialogue seemed to be the complaints from a surprisingly large number of people. It really caught me off guard because I liked what I had seen.

But my reaction was modest compared to how it affected Redford. As we read the negative comments, his face got tighter and more severe, and finally he called a halt to our reading of the comments. It was clear that some changes were needed. He thanked us all for being there, stood up and walked away.

It took a year for the movie to appear, and when it did, it was much different from what our test audience had seen. Quietly, Redford had thoroughly re-edited the movie. Good thing he did, too, because when the dust settled, he had transformed an ugly duckling into a graceful swan, and in the process created a classic.

At this time, the mid 1960s through the mid 1970s, I was pleased whenever I could get a movie role. But my basic go-to work was episodic television because the opportunities were more plentiful and it seemed as if new shows were being developed almost weekly. There were only three major networks at this time, CBS, NBC and ABC, unlike today where cable has opened things up so outlets like Netflix, Hulu and Amazon have given a wider choice of programs.

Sometimes, the networks themselves would develop their own shows, but often the networks relied on independent production companies to develop a series idea and present it to them in the form of a pilot. The pilot episode established the world and the major characters of the potential series. If the network liked the pilot, often swayed by test audience reaction, they would order additional episodes for future airing.

Not every pilot sold, of course, and this made the entire process of story development, casting, costuming and overall production uncertain, at best. Yet this was also, the golden age for the television pilot. It seemed as if someone, somewhere was putting together a pilot almost every week. And for a working actor like me, that was just fine. Looking back now, I realize that no six month period went by without my acting in a pilot somewhere.

It almost got routine I'd get a call from my agent, saying something like, "They want you over at CBS," and then briefly describing the pilot they were putting together. I'd ask him who was directing, who was casting, who was in the cast, and invariably, I'd have worked with a couple of them.

"They say anything about my reading for the part?" I'd inquire, and usually the response was, "The producer/director/casting director knows you. No problem there." And that would be that, without an audition or fingernail biting.

One of the pilots I remember particularly well was for Bing Crosby Productions in the mid 1960s. The series would be called *Rachel's Camp* and it was set in the time of the Gold Rush in California during the 19th century. I played Cain, a gunfighter with a mysterious past and opposite me was a good guy character played by Richard Bradford, an English actor who developed a successful career both on the screen and in live theater.

We shot the pilot in Sonora, California, north of San Francisco, and I remember being surprised, almost shocked, really, at how costly the production became. From elaborate physical sets to ornate costuming to omnipresent horses and carriages, we guessed the pilot, itself, must have had a budget of at least $500,000, certainly a lot of money for an untried show in those days.

And we all thought we had a winner. Bradford and I worked well together, and the story line was intriguing and provocative.

"Everybody loves stories about finding gold," Bradford told me. "People relate because there's a 'gold bug' in all of us, and then you have the gun fighting and the horse chases."

Sadly, though, the pilot never sold to the networks. We figured it was probably because the production costs would be so high, week after week. And it wasn't fresh enough to attract its own audience while competing with the bevy of westerns that filled up the network schedule at that time. For me, though, what made it sad was confirmation of what more experienced actors had already told me: "Most pilots don't sell. Get used to it!"

But you never really do because each time you're cast in a new pilot, you're filled with a surge of enthusiasm and you poke around, looking for those special details that could mean this pilot will be "different." It's your wishful thinking, of course, along with your sense of reason that a well-scripted, well-acted, well-directed story will achieve inevitable success.

A year after Rachel's Camp, my agent called. "NBC wants you for something they're calling *Two Men and a Girl in a Meat Grinder*, which sure is a mouthful!" I played a storefront lawyer, working in the ghetto, which is what the show called the meat grinder.' I helped people who couldn't help themselves, at the time a very 1960s story idea. My co-star was Billy D. Williams and the girl was Hildy Brooks. From the first day, the three of us really hit it off. Hildy had a lot of perky energy, Billy D. was a fine actor, and as important as anything else was that I loved the idea of the show: a black guy, a white guy and a girl doing good deeds and helping other people.

But that series title bugged us. I remember my agent's final comment as I left his office for NBC: "Get them to change that name. It sounds like a comedy."

The director was Allen Baron, a television veteran with decades of experience, and he beat me to the punch when it came to the series title. He invited the three leads to his home to "tear into the script," as he liked to say.

One of the first things he said was, "The title? Forget it. We're calling it *Risk*. Same story line, same everything else." Then, we sat around his ample living room for two long days, running over the scenes in the pilot, talking about the characters and agreeing the new title made a lot more sense. By the time we had wrapped things up, all of us felt quite good about what we were doing. Billy D. and Hildy and I got along as if we had been working together for years, the entire show was unfolding beautifully and just before we left, Allen Baron said to us, "I can't believe this won't sell!"

A few moments later, he took me aside and added quietly, "This is going to make you a big star!" It was that word again.

Alas, this would not be a career breakthough. At first, we were riding high. NBC liked the pilot and authorized several additional shows to be produced and aired. But suddenly, after the fifth show, we were informed that production was shutting down. We were canceled with no warning, no time to prepare. When that happens, they rarely tell you why. So often, it's a business decision that flows back and forth between the production people and the financial people and never reaches the actors. However, we did have an idea from what Allen Baron found out when speaking to one of the producers.

"The time slot," he said. "We couldn't make it work." CBS had a popular show, *Eight Is Enough*, about a father and his eight independent-minded kids and how they survived living with one another and grew into adulthood. NBC saw *Risk* as a challenge to this long-running CBS family sitcom, and they slotted us opposite it on the weekly schedule.

Unfortunately, by the fifth episode in our series, it was clear the ratings were going in the wrong direction, and *Eight Is Enough* was not losing its audience.

Allen Baron said it for all of us when I saw him shortly after we'd been canceled: "It was a good show, damn it!"

The next year, I slid back into the "western" scene with a new pilot, this time following the life of Joaquin Murrieta, an outlaw during the time of the California Gold Rush who was known as the "Mexican Robin Hood" for his zeal in protecting the "have-nots" from the "haves."

Ricardo Montalban played Murrieta, and there were four other leads who formed his gang. I played Arkansas, a feisty, young gunfighter, slick and arrogant, always on the edge of a confrontation. Then, there was Roosevelt Grier, the huge, former NFL football player who played a runaway slave and joined the gang to escape capture. The third member of the gang was my old pal Slim Pickens, who played a slick con man known as Three-Finger Jack. The fourth member of the gang was Shad Clay, played by Earl Holliman, a notorious and highly dangerous gunfighter.

As we worked on the pilot, all of us felt a sense of camaraderie and confidence. The cast was terrific and the theme of the underdog prevailing over a hard-hearted establishment and the romantic notion of the sensitive outlaw made us think the series had all the earmarks of success.

But here again, our confidence was misplaced. The pilot didn't sell. No one gave us a reason. For a couple of days, all of us were feeling more confused than angry. How could a show with *this* cast not sell?

Then, one of the assistant directors mentioned that they were rerunning the pilot for a couple of independent producers who were looking at it as a made-for-television movie.

"I can get you into the screening," the assistant director said, and I thought it might be interesting to see the pilot from beginning to end. It was something I'd never actually done with that show, in spite of being one of the leads. Generally, you checked the shooting schedule, you learned your lines, you followed the director's instructions, and then you waited for your next scene, which could be days away. Once your work was finished, you went off to the next acting gig, if you had one. There was no sense in waiting around until the pilot went through post-production and was ready for viewing, That could take weeks, and who's got that amount of time to sit around?

We had done five episodes of the Joaquin Murrieta project before we were canceled. The finished pilot was ready for us to view. The leading characters all agreed to see the screening and found seats in the back of a studio screening room.

Within ten minutes, we had the answer why the series didn't sell to the network. The script simply sucked, so to speak, pure and simple. It was contrived, lacked authenticity and was replete with cringe-worthy lines. I never gave a thought to how effective or how authentic the lines might sound when I performed them. I assumed, as did the other actors, that we were professionals doing what professionals did, performing a professionally written, directed and produced story. I never gave a thought to judging the quality of the script. My job was to portray what the script showed, and the only emotion I recall at the time was excitement about having a role in the pilot with other talented actors. My job certainly wasn't to judge the script as I read my lines or to have any say in how the script might need changing.

But after those opening ten minutes in the screening room, we looked at one another, and we knew without saying a word... there was something wrong, the show was boring, the lines were boring, and the characters... it was tough to work up a connection with them.

But we did achieve a happy ending of sorts. Those independent producers saw something in the opening half hour of the pilot, and they decided to go forward with a made-for-television movie, based on that.

A week after I walked out of the screening room depressed and embarrassed by what I had seen, my agent called. "Get your bags packed, my friend. You're off to Durango, Mexico!"

Not only had the producers decided to get started right away, they also wanted to do the filming in Mexico. It would be the same cast as the pilot and the same general story about Murrieta who fought for and protected the weak. There was a new title, *The Desperate Mission*.

We spent a month in Durango filming the movie, and it gave me a chance to get to know Slim Pickens better. I relish the memory because we clicked when it came to our attitudes about acting and performing. Acting was our day job, but it didn't consume us, the way it sometimes did with younger actors. Life was not a series of ascending steps towards some actor's nirvana.

The first thing that set Slim Pickens apart was how he got his name. When he was a young man and carried the name Louis Lindley, he interviewed for a job with a rodeo that came through his California town. He was fairly tall and quite scrawny, but he had a strange kind of magnetism. The interviewer told him he wasn't sure he could use him, that there was "slim pickings" when it came to working for the rodeo. But then he ran his eyes over Slim's thin body and he got an idea.

"You ever done stuff in front of an audience?" the interviewer asked.

Slim shrugged, not sure what the interviewer meant.

"You mind being laughed at?"

Slim said that didn't bother him. And so Slim was hired as a rodeo clown, which he did for the next twenty years. He thought about his name, Louis Lindley, and somehow that just didn't fit the role of a rodeo clown. He thought back to the interviewer and his comment about "slim pickings" when it came to rodeo jobs. What if he took *that* as his name. Slim dropped the letter 'G" at the end and made himself the perfect name for a cowboy actor.

Slim was a fun-loving man. His years on the hard-living rodeo circuit, as well as his acquired skills in whipping up raucous crowd reactions to his antics in the rodeo ring kept things loose and active on the set. He liked to drink, though never while he was working. But come evening, after the days shooting had wrapped, you generally found him in the middle of some outlandish idea which usually meant following him and continuing the party.

One evening, after a couple of hours of drinking, Slim suggested, "Let's take the honey wagon into town and find us some girls." The honey wagon was a large vehicle, somewhat like an over-sized bus, with six compartments that we used as dressing rooms along with a separate bathroom. It was what a lot of production teams used when they went on location. Each lead actor had a dressing room and could count on a bit of privacy, though you had to fight through the musty, sour-tinged odors that seemed to stick to the walls of your compartment. Our vehicle had certainly seen better days.

Nevertheless, Slim spoke to the driver, and he agreed to drive us. So off we went, each of us in our dressing room, and after a few miles, we reached the nearest town, a nondescript four block long place with high adobe walls. Halfway down the main street, now in darkness, was a large neon sign, the only light on the street, and it blinked "Bar" and "Mexicano/Americano" outside a two storey structure.

The driver pointed. " *Las chicas!*"

Slim was the first one off the honey-wagon. "Man, we are here!" he shouted and led us into the bar.

After a bit of financial negotiating, the girls inside were delighted to join us on the honey wagon, and four hours later, Slim led us, stumbling, off the honey wagon back at where we were staying. Though he never actually uttered it, I'm sure Slim carried the same thought in his alcohol-saturated mind as each of us did while weaving our way to bed. Don't tell the producers or director about the honeys who were in the wagon.

In 1974, I was contacted by Aaron Spelling to work on still another pilot. Spelling and I went back several years, and by the early 70s, he had become one of the most active television producers in Hollywood. I had worked on several of his shows by this time, including *Mod Squad*, *Charlie's Angels* and *The Rookies*.

But this new one was quite different. I was one of the leads in a half-hour show about two policemen in a helicopter. It was called

Chopper One and my co-star was Dirk Benedict, who would later star in Spelling's popular *The A-Team*. In the show, one of us flew the helicopter, and the other observed as we prowled above the dramatically challenging landscape of Southern California. The pilot sold to ABC, which made us all quite happy, and they paired us with another half-hour show, *Firehouse*, about a Los Angeles fire company, to create a solid one-hour, thematically linked dramatic experience.

Chopper One didn't last very long, just 13 episodes. This was the time of the first Arab oil embargo, and in the middle of our production schedule, fuel prices suddenly shot through the roof. Since the helicopter and our flying about in it were crucial to maintaining the show's story line, the program budget couldn't survive the sudden escalation of fuel prices. But one thing that sticks out about the experience was that my son, Tysun, was born during the running of the show. And before we were forced to shut down, I made up and circulated a birth announcement which showed our chopper, hovering and holding a baby carriage off the ground with Tysun's sweet face peering out of the carriage.

As I think back to those days, I wonder if we're better off now. It's certainly more complicated with all those cable channels also producing as well as showing programs. Independent producers are able to show their work at myriad film festivals now available across the globe.

Sadly, they don't do as many pilots as they used to do. When we lived and worked in the world of the television pilot, we had a level of excitement I'm not sure today's actors can truly appreciate.

There were only three TV networks. But with a score of actors vying for roles, there were many creative ideas that at least had a chance to see the light of day.

Chapter Nine

Michael and Me

ONE FINE SPRING day during my episodic television period, I found myself tooling through elegant Holmby Hills in West Los Angeles, on my way to Michael Crichton's house. We had just wrapped a two-hour television movie based on his book, *Binary*, and he and I had formed a blossoming friendship. He had learned about my early study of architecture at the University of Kansas.

He told me the subject had always intrigued him. "I love the blending of design with three-dimensional creation," he said. "Your imagination becomes a working tool and provides so much for so many people." He smiled a little. "It can even become a work of art, sometimes."

It was the idea of architecture as a work of art that prompted me to drive to his house that day.

"You ever hear of Richard Neutra?" Michael had asked me.

"Of course," I said, though admittedly, my knowledge was limited to the fact he was originally from Austria, had acquired an international reputation for uncomplicated, open-air architectural design and had worked with my early hero, Frank Lloyd Wright.

"He designed my house," Michael offered, adding that Neutra had had an office in Los Angeles for years and was currently designing custom villas and multi-level country homes across the face of Europe. A few years earlier, though, Neutra had busied himself with designing homes in the Los Angeles area and had acquired a local reputation. His designs, Michael said, were geometrically acute, sharp lines, clean and airy which seemingly soared to the sky.

"It all looks so simple," Michael had chuckled, "but you and I know better, don't we?"

Indeed we did. It's the same with many masters of creative arts. What looks simple masks a complex thought process. Take Picasso's sketch work. A few barely connected lines combined to show a portrait and a distinct attitude. Or take Robert Frost's meaningful words, "Good fences make good neighbors." Five words convey a full philosophy.

And so it was with Richard Neutra's architectural designs, open, flexible and easily modified to cope with a finicky client. His work was more about personal comfort than rigidly classical in nature. Yet, no line, no corner, no arch, no wall seemed purposeless. With Michael's home, the geometric lines were clearly defined, and despite the seeming simplicity of those lines, there was nothing cold or uninspiring about the design. Somehow, it felt comfortable within those walls.

As he showed me around the house, I noticed that he had to duck to get through doorways. "I guess Neutra didn't figure someone like me might own one of his houses," he said ruefully. Michael was six feet, nine inches tall, and the tops of the doorways were a bit below that.

"Every time I walk through a doorway, I have to remember to duck," he said, "so I'm going to rebuild the doorways another foot higher."

When he said it, though, there was sadness on his face, and I understood right away.

"Imagine," he said, "you're living in a house designed by one of the century's great architects, and you just don't fit. It makes me so sad," he added.

Michael had written *Binary* when he attended Harvard Medical School, and it was labeled a techno-thriller because it combined chemistry gone wild with elements of mystery and suspense. The story line portrayed a millionaire who hated America. He concocted a poisonous chemical formula that could kill millions of people, and the hero of the tale tried to prevent that from happening. Michael wrote this book under the pen name John Lange, and when it was published, it received modest praise and no major book awards.

But Barry Diller at ABC had already seen the book before it was published and wanted it as a movie-of-the-week. Michael, who long had a desire to get involved with movies, agreed to sell the television movie rights, provided he could direct the movie, as well. At first, Diller refused; after all, Michael Crichton had never directed a movie before, never been around Hollywood. But Michael stood his ground and finally they came to a compromise: Michael could direct the movie if Diller selected an experienced screenwriter to do the script. Diller arranged for Robert Dozier, who had numerous screen writing credits, to come aboard, and soon, things were under way.

I remember Michael chuckling at how things had turned out. "My book, I direct the movie, but someone else does the script based on my book. Crazy!"

The first thing ABC did was to change the title of the show. Instead of Michael's title, *Binary*, they decided to call the movie *Pursuit*. And it would have a solid, professional cast. The lead, the scientific mastermind who wanted to poison millions of people was played by veteran actor E.G. Marshall, and the intelligence agent who tried to stop him was played by Ben Gazzara.

Since this was Michael's first directing gig, he was quite nervous, and during the first few hours of the shoot, that nervousness communicated itself to the cast. I sensed what was going on and figured Michael might need a friendly face in the midst of his uncertainty.

So, during a of break that first day, I made a point of seeking Michael out, and asked if there was anything I could do to help things along. I offered myself as a sounding board for what he was trying to do.

He said, "I could use some help with the long shots. My angles seem off, and I'm not sure why." I told him that if he shot "down" rather than "across," he might find it easier, and sure enough that seemed to make a difference. Soon, he was asking my advice on other shots, although there was no question he retained control of the overall shoot. As we talked, I found myself really liking this gangly, gentle person. He was a mild, unassuming man. He avoided confrontation whenever he could and the idea of "making any waves" seemed very much out of character. He liked to be alone and he loved his work. He was definitely not a Hollywood type who loved parties and schmoozing. Almost everyone who met him liked him.

He admitted to me he was having trouble communicating with several of the actors, particularly Ben Gazzara. They listened to him, he said, but then they'd ignore him on camera..

I told him I was having the same problem with Gazzara. "The guy's so damn uncommunicative between takes. We're like strangers seconds after the camera stops." This reminded me of my experiences with and reactions to Vince Edwards back when I was working on the *Ben Casey*. There was no sense of a shared experience. It was cold and unfriendly, almost as if we were acting "machines" and not living, breathing humans.

As Ben Gazzara's partner on screen, I would often sit next to him in the patrol car. Yet when we weren't shooting, he'd never exchange a word with me. He remained silent as if I was not there. At first, I thought it might have something to do with his acting technique, similar to the way method actors obsessed and worked themselves up to portraying a role.

But Michael told me he was having the same trouble with Gazzara. "I can't seem to reach him," he said, adding the guy was simply "uncommunicative."

Sometimes you simply have to roll with the idiosyncrasies of the other actors and work around what you're faced with. Michael asked me to help explain to Gazzara and the other actors what he wanted to appear on screen.

"Actors understand other actors," he said to me. "You speak the same language and I'm the new guy around here."

So that was what happened, and in the process, Michael and I developed a friendship. I wouldn't say Gazzara and the others were joyful when I interpreted Michael's directing instructions for them. But there was begrudging acceptance that Michael was the director and I was his chosen spokesperson.

Actually, Michael did have an important ability when it came to directing. He had the skill to make you relax, and he wasn't someone with an opinion on everything. Perhaps it was his uncertain level of confidence at this early stage in his career, but it was clear from the outset that he trusted the professionals he worked with. E.G. Marshall and Ben Gazzara, had instant respect from Michael. He gave the cast the benefit of the doubt when it came to knowing their craft. He wouldn't put you through some kind of "skill test," such as an audition or a special "reading" before accepting you into the cast. He figured the actors would do what they were supposed to do, and he wasn't going to second guess their judgment.

"I just guide them along," he would say again and again, and he tried to keep it uncomplicated. "I like that one, so print it," was his quiet mantra.

Not long after that evening at his house, Michael called and said he had written the script for a low-budget, erotic suspense story. "I want you to headline it," he said, "The lead is a great part, and you'd be perfect playing it." The movie was budgeted for a mere $150,000, a personal friend would produce it and try to sell it to the studios.

"I'm calling it *Extreme Close-up*," Michael said. "It's about a newsman doing an expose on news outlets in the business of bugging and snooping to get their stories." I played the newsman, who worked with a cameraman, played by James Watson. We set about interviewing people who pushed the envelope on bugging and snooping. Along the way, we got involved with those who sold equipment to the buggers and snoopers. We investigated where they found the equipment and how much they paid for it.

And then the plot shifted. My character, John Norman, progressed from straight newsman to becoming one of the characters in the story he had originally targeted. In short, my character becomes the object of the story he had been pursuing.

John got fascinated with the surveillance equipment and tested it and then decided to try it out, in the name of satisfying his own curiosity, of course. Gradually, as his skill and obsession with the equipment grew, he began spying on an attractive woman, oblivious to his original purpose as newsman. The man who wanted to write about Peeping Toms had now become one.

Though this was Michael's screenplay, he didn't direct it, leaving that to young French director, Jeannot Szwarc, whom I enjoyed working with. Still, from the beginning, it was called Michael Crichton's movie, and that's what built up my expectation that we had a real winner. Michael had already achieved major success with *Westworld* and *The Andromeda Strain*. and some were even comparing him with the young Orson Welles.

I worked very hard on this movie, but it never seemed to gain traction in the pre-release period, and before it was released publicly, the producers sold it into the "B" movie market, where a less discerning audience awaited. It was given an "R" rating, and very unfortunately, its title was changed to *Sex Through a Window*.

I had a chance to watch the movie a short while after we wrapped the production, and I came away understanding why it failed to generate the buzz I was expecting. The problem was a lot of flash and not much fire, a good idea without corresponding substance. All of us, the director, Michael and me, had put a lot into making the movie work, but the characters were card-board-like, and the dialogue was strained. I suppose you could also argue that the tight budget and the fact that we sped the production along very quickly probably didn't help. But the story idea was clever, and all of us liked working with Michael.

One sweet memory does come out of the movie, though, and it eases my overall disappointment a bit. A couple of times when Michael had invited me to his house, Helene came along, and one day he asked her if she'd like a walk-on part in the movie. Our first child, Sky, had just been born, and Michael suggested Helene bring the baby to the set. He'd found a baby carriage, and Helene was be filmed wheeling Sky in the background of a couple of scenes. Michael enjoyed setting this up for us and Helene was pleased to get to know him and the filming went smoothly.

At the time, his novel, *Terminal Man*, had just been published, and one day, while we were still in production on his movie, Michael arrived on set with a copy of the book for me. He had inscribed inside the front cover, "For Jim McMullan who seems to be involved with the simultaneous birth of more first children than is humanly possible. Thank you. Michael."

By the late 1970s, Michael's movie *Westworld*, which he'd both written and directed, had become a major hit. The story involved an amusement park, a kind of virtual Disneyland, where visitors lived out their fantasies by assuming any identity they wished and then interacting with specially created androids who assisted in developing those fantasies. Instead of seeking out a standard amusement park thrill-ride, visitors went to a dressing room, chose a costume and then move to a specially designed location where the androids would be waiting. Depending upon the visitors' fantasies, the scene might resemble a saloon from an Old West town or an Alaskan gold mining camp or even an opulent, Gay 90s robber baron's drawing room. But the key was that the androids challenged the visitors to a gun fight or other type of physical altercation, and in subduing the androids the visitor, hopefully, lived out his or her greatest fantasy.

In Michael's story, however, the androids go off script and begin attacking the visitors, and everything goes haywire. It's a classic Michael Crichton story line. Just when you think science and technology are under your control, something happens which creates havoc and establishes that all forms of matter are only reliable up to a point. And one should never assume that having power over anything means possessing total control, as well.

Michael called me one day and said that MGM was interested in remaking *Westworld* into a prime-time television series, involving an evil character taking over the androids and a good guy character trying to stop him each week.

"They want to call it *Beyond Westworld*, and I suggested you for the good guy lead," he said. The television show would pick up the story from the point where the evil character had destroyed the original Westworld because he hadn't approved of how the androids had been treated there. And now, he was bent on taking over the entire world through his androids. "You'll need to read for the part," Michael added, "and this is only a pilot. But I don't think there's a problem with your getting the role." There wasn't, and within a matter of weeks, we were on the road to production.

I played John Moore, an android expert and troubleshooter. This was before the days when "techie" would be a familiar word to explain someone's technological skill set. But I suppose you could call my character a "techie" because of his familiarity with the inner workings of the androids. My evil counterpart was Simon Quaid, who was played by James Wainwright.

Each week, Quaid sent out his androids to create havoc somewhere, and each week, my partners and I were dispatched to stop him. When Michael and I first discussed the show and my role, I expected Quaid would be played by an older man, a mature character, gray-haired, lined face, hooded, rheumy eyes and so on. But Wainwright turned out to be about my age, clean-cut, though he did have an evil look about him. I always wondered whether he had sufficient credibility as an "evil genius."

In the pilot, Simon Quaid installed an android among the crew on a Navy submarine, and the android's mission was to take over the submarine and wreak destruction on shore. My office got wind of the plot, and I was dispatched, along with my partners and an android "expert" (played by Bill Jordan) to find the android and prevent the looming disaster.

A helicopter dropped us onto the deck of an actual submarine, which was definitely a new experience for me. And we spent the balance of the pilot searching through the sub's interior and interviewing the crew to uncover the android. Some false starts and missed clues later, I finally identified the android, and we had a climactic physical battle in the sub's torpedo room.

Eventually, I overpowered him and stuffed him in a torpedo tube. Then, as a final act, I hit the torpedo launch button, and with a *whoooooooshhh*, the android was shot out of the tube and dis-integrates in the unforgiving ocean.

When the pilot was finished, we were quite excited about its prospects. It had the Michael Crichton stamp of genius, and a story line that built upon the undeniable success of a very popular and recent movie. In fact, Helene and I talked MGM into letting us use a screening room to show the pilot to our friends and some of the cast and technical crew. We turned it into a celebratory event, a party with drinks and food, and we were thrilled with comments from the audience after the screening. We were rewarded with words like "great drama," "clever story idea." and "should make a fantastic series." Sure enough, within a matter of days, CBS came back and said they loved the pilot and wanted thirteen episodes, a full season's commitment. However, they inserted a clause that allowed them to order less shows, if they chose. But this contractual issue barely registered with us. We were so sure, so sure.

Sometimes, in the television business, unlike the movies, things can happen so fast that you end up getting ahead of yourself and end on a limb without any support. That's what happened with *Beyond Westworld*. We were very excited that the pilot had been received so well, but no one, not the producers or the writers, had thought, what if the pilot gets accepted? What then? No one had prepared any follow-up scripts. No one had thought through where the evolving story line would go. No one had arranged a studio space. No one, in fact, had thought beyond the pilot. Suddenly, we had to do some scrambling because CBS was not going to let us take the time on story development and characterizations that marked the pilot.

The producers rushed around seeking writers who could turn out material in hours and days instead of weeks. But that can be a formula for disaster because process (getting the writing done in a hurry) starts to control product (the authenticity and quality of the script). What you end up with is writing that just doesn't work very well. It reads contrived and undramatic.

Simultaneous to the script problems, my co-star, James Wainwright, was unhappy with his perceived treatment on the set and in the show itself. I think he saw himself as the actual star of the show, the top guy, rather than as my co-star sharing top billing. The producers had made it clear but Wainwright continued to have a problem with that.

For example, when I was assigned a dressing room, the producers said to choose whatever colors and style I wished. So, I opted for something Japanese with delicately designed, 125 filmy curtains and smooth, blonde bamboo. One day, Wainwright came by and pointedly examined how I'd furnished my space.

"Shit," he uttered, "this is nicer than mine." He stormed off, went straight to the producers and demanded his dressing room be upgraded and redesigned. They accommodated him that time, but it turned out to be the beginning of a problem rather than the end of one. Soon, he got picky about his costuming and which wardrobe mistress would be assigned to him. Then, he objected to the scripts themselves, complaining I had "better" lines than he did, or "more" lines or "greater" screen time. He demanded that things be changed in his favor, and if the producers didn't comply, he'd give less than a full performance and make things really awkward on set, forcing the overall production to suffer. His demands were met about half the time.

Not too surprisingly, I didn't like working with him. But the professional in me wouldn't let things fall apart, even Wainwright was doing his best to do so. Still, it was difficult to keep the drama flowing, to maintain authenticity in the characterization when your inner self struggled to paper over resentment towards your co-star. The energy between us before the cameras was not strong, and that sent a negative signal to the producers.

But we had that commitment from CBS for 13 weeks, and that's what drove us forward, even if the sparks we felt from the pilot had died away. One day, after we had wrapped the fifth show in the series, the producers called the cast and crew together on the studio floor. A sense of anticipation gripped us as we exchanged questioning looks, but one glance at the producers' faces, and you knew what was coming.

"We have some bad news, folks," said the spokesman. "We're not finishing the series. In fact, we're done as of right now. It's a network call, and CBS has decided to move on." Then, after the initial shock wore off, the spokesman added, "We're all real sorry. It was a good show, and you should be proud of the work you've done."

In ten minutes, we had become a memory, and it had happened stunningly fast. Months of hard work, excitement about working with Michael and turning out a really good pilot, getting a 13 week commitment from CBS, allowing myself to dream that this time, my starring role would vault me higher than I had ever gone had all ended after just five weeks into the season.

I remember standing with Michael afterwards, just the two of us at the edge of the empty set after everyone had left.

"I'm really sorry, Jim. I had hope for this one," he said I told him how grateful I'd been for his thinking of me when he'd put the show idea together.

"You were great," he said. "Maybe we can do it again."

Alas, we never did, and when he died so young, at age 66 in 2008, I mourned him as a brother.

Chapter Ten

The Soaps

IN THE EARLY 1980s I was suffering a condition which actors call "between shows," meaning I had no work, even though I was available and eager to perform. All working actors contend with this condition. It's less an embarrassment than an annoyance because it rarely signifies a judgment on your talent. Instead, it's a reflection of a marketplace where, at least temporarily, there are too many actors who are your type and too few roles. Every actor knows being cast is a fluid situation. It requires patience for and faith in the future. It's a challenge because remaining positive can be a major test when your bank balance keeps dropping.

Actors resort to numerous and sometimes surprising alternatives to weather the "between shows" struggle. In the 1990s, for example, I spent a year or so as a yard maintenance worker, trimming trees, raking leaves, cutting grass and the like, even though I didn't like it. I know of other actors who became interstate bus drivers or vocational/technical instructors or restaurant cooks or real estate agents. You do what you have to do to survive. But the wise actors never stray far from the acting world where you maintained your contacts, where you absorbed what the "trades" such as the *Hollywood Reporter* had to offer each day. You kept your physical appearance at its highest level because you never really knew what might come your way at any moment.

My agent called one day, and I could sense frustration in his tone because we hadn't been having much luck with auditions or with fitting me into available roles. It had been months since I had been cast in anything, and I was beginning to wonder where my future lay.

"We've got to think more creatively," the agent, whose name was Morrie, said. "Five years ago, we had choices, but today..." He left me with a verbal shoulder shrug.

"I'm not tough to please, Morrie."

"Maybe it's time to try something different."

For an instant, I feared he was going to cut me adrift, so his next words really surprised me. "What if, have you ever thought about the soaps?"

There was silence. Before I could respond, he pushed his words out rapidly. "They're big now. Lots of good acting spots. The networks love them. An actor gets a sustaining role, and bingo, they're set for years. Years, Jim!" Morrie's voice blossomed with enthusiasm. "I mean, it could be a career!"

The soaps. I had never worked on any of them, although I knew they were a world of their own. They even had their own annual awards show, the Daytime Emmys. Stories abounded about actors who went to work on the soaps and never appeared on any prime time network shows again. There were time demands because the popular soaps were on the air five times a week. And the daytime audience for the soaps was far different than the evening audience for prime time shows.

I'd resisted working on the soaps for a long time, and agents before Morrie had tried to recruit me for them. I remember years earlier when I was hanging around with Jimmy Caan, and an agent had suggested I consider the work. Jimmy, whose laser-like career interest was always on the movies, said to me, "No, no, no, no, Jim, don't do it. Do movies. Stay with movies." At the time, movies were considered the top of the mountain and appearing in prime time on one of the networks was the next rung down. Far down the list were the soaps, and at that point in my career, I decided that there was no way I was going to let myself sink that far down.

Over the years, I had learned quite a bit about the soaps, most of it disagreeable, even seriously off-putting. True, some of the better soaps, such as *The Young and the Restless* and *The Days of Our Lives* had been around for decades, so they were established and reliable. An actor with an ongoing role could expect to spend years on screen. But the work can be quite difficult, and if the show is relatively new and trying to find its market, you can be treated like a piece of meat, moved around like you're a pawn on a board and not granted a lot of respect by the producers.

Everything happens so fast with the soaps. Usually, they shoot a show in one day. The rehearsals are quick and superficial, and the key is to keep things as uncomplicated as possible.

This means that they use a lot of head shots, and the actors don't move around the set much.

Thus, the director isn't pushed to become more creative with camera work, and the actors aren't pushed to create more meaningful, more impactful characters. Often, the day's shoot is a set that represents perhaps a living room or an office, and most of the entire episode is just a few locations.

If you're one of the leads on the soap, imagine learning new lines each day, rehearsing and performing something different each day and struggling to meet the show's inexorable dead-line each day.

All these thoughts swirled through my head as Morrie waited for my response. The way I felt about the soaps, if I did come around, could I look myself in the mirror without cringing?

Would that turn my acting sour? "I don't know, Morrie," I said honestly. "What kind of price would I pay for this so-called career in a soap?"

"You're over-thinking. And anyway, if you don't like it, you can always walk away."

We left it there. Morrie promised to check on what work there might be in the soaps. He had no commitment from me about signing on.

It was less than 24 hours later when he called me.

"Got something interesting here," Morrie said. True, it would fall into the soap category, but it was hardly vintage stuff. "They're calling it *New Day in Eden*. It's to be the first R-rated soap and it'll appear on Showtime. Think of that!" He said they would be regularly showing frontal nudity, though none below the waist. The show would carry an aura of permissive sex.

"People are excited about the show," Morrie insisted, "and I think I can get you a leading role, if you're interested." He added that it was slotted to be shown late at night and to a pay cable. "We're still feeling our way, here," he emphasized, not recognizing his ironic choice of words.

I didn't know what to say. I had always supported any breakthrough in free expression, and here we had a major step forward. Still, it was the soaps, the daily grind, a daytime audience, pedestrian directing, uninspired scripts, even if the actors were flashing the cameras with some of their clothes off.

"Tell me about the role," I asked Morrie. He said I'd play the patriarch of a family that had made a fortune in the electronics business. I had several kids who were always getting into trouble from which I would try to rescue them. The story was set in a sleepy hamlet called Eden, and the episodes regularly contained sex and rape and assault and murder.

"I'd call it soft porn," Morrie added, "very racy and all that." He said the R-rating would certainly bring attention to the show, and it could have a future because it was more interesting than what was in the other soaps.

And it would be a one hour show each week, instead of the usual half-hour soap episodes, which meant the stories would have more depth and the characters would be more dimensional.

The money, however, would not be great. Even as one of the leads, I'd only get $750 per show, and that was one-third of what I was used to getting on any regular network show, even if I only made a one-day appearance there.

But my "between shows" condition wasn't getting better, money was money, and working sure beat sitting and waiting for the uncooperative phone to ring. So, I said okay and not with a great deal of enthusiasm, I admit. But at least I'd be part of a ground-breaking television concept, and I was curious about how the producers were going to pull this off.

Right away, it was clear this would be no walk in the park. The work was hard and long, and at times it became an endurance test. Each day, you'd had to be familiar with 20-30 pages of script, often learning new lines of dialogue. And while that did get easier the more you did it, it always required time and close attention. I spent every weekend, often deep into the nights, learning my lines for the next week, and I actually had nightmares about the pressure, it was so intense. Sometimes, we shot late into the evening. But there was an unexpected benefit: The daily demands actually helped me to improve my line memorization skills and be better prepared when in front of the camera.

Still, it was pretty much a shoestring budget. The producers didn't have a lot of money and there were no stars and no dressing rooms. They gave you a hook to hang your clothes on.

We did shoot in a legitimate Hollywood studio, though it wasn't one anyone was familiar with, but the overall experience did increase my ability to "turn on" my acting quicker and more thoroughly. The nudity, actually, was done quite discreetly, The scenes were brief, done with dim lighting and often, the nudity was shown in profile.

The show lasted one season, and I was in 26 of the 33 episodes. By the end, I was tired of it all. The intensity of the schedule was so different from anything I had ever done. My character was always involved in high drama, sometimes having to bail his kids out of jail or rescue them from some other kind of trouble. After a while, there was a sameness to it all that made it almost boring. Privately, though, I was pleased to be a part of something that broke new ground, as this show did, and as for the "racy" portions of the show, I'm never one to make quick, moral judgments, so long as what occurs on screen contributes to the progress of the story. Personally, I was a spectator rather than a participant when the R-rated story portions appeared, and that was fine with me. People magazine discussed the level of my participation in the nudity by writing, "By the season's end, Bryan Lewis [my character] will have kept his clothes on in every episode, a fact that disgruntles the actor who plays him." Then they quoted my words: "I just wish he could get out of the office. I'm tired of sitting behind a desk and staring at the green carpet. When I finally do get into a bed, it will probably be with my tie on."

They made it sound like I wanted to run around as naked as a jay bird.

An interesting aspect to the soaps is that the underlying story line is projected well into the future. That allows for flexibility with the characters and with what can happen, should something unexpected crop up. For example, an actor could get seriously ill and be unable to play his or her part for awhile. With some deft rewriting, the character could be "written out" of the plot for a period of time, while the other story threads continue to develop. Nothing in the soaps, not the characters, story line or even the setting is written in stone. All is subject to change in order to accommodate the demands of the cast and the show, itself.

But sometimes, even though the need for change could be staring the producers right in the face, they decide that altering the script to make a change or two creates more havoc than not doing so. And in the end, the sanctity of the approved script becomes affirmed.

Two years after *Eden*, I decided to try another soap. This time, however, I aimed higher. I played a character on one of the gold standard soaps, *The Young and the Restless*. The show had been around since 1972, and more than 11,000 episodes had aired. So, its audience and time slot were very reliable and secure. The show was set in the fictitious town of Genoa City, Wisconsin, and I played Brent Davis, a golf pro, who returned to town to reconnect with his daughter, Ashley, after he had left her mother and moved away years before. The problem was that most people in town thought Ashley was the daughter of another man, so my character's credibility as the father was seriously challenged since he hadn't been on the scene for years. But Brent was determined to let the world know Ashley was *his* daughter.

The projected script had me as a drunk and a troublemaker, leading a dissipated life and screwing up things for everybody. My initial contract was for six months, rather than for a specific number of episodes. The plan was to eventually kill me off after those six months.

Within my first week on the show, I felt some of the same pressure I had endured on *Eden*. While I had gotten better at handling the speedy learning of lines and once-over-lightly production approaches, it still wasn't a lot of fun. I noticed that some of the actors had been with the show for more than ten years, and they'd made a career for themselves.

One day, shortly after I joined the show, I talked with one of the old-timers, and I mentioned the pressure of learning so many lines so quickly. He nodded at a nearby teleprompter.

"Who needs to memorize?" he asked. "If you can read, you're golden." It turned out that he never memorized anything. Over the years, he'd become a master at using the teleprompter.

You could never tell from watching the screen that he was using the prompter because it never looked like he was reading anything at all. He had it all figured out.

"I have my own life outside the studio, away from the cameras," he told me, "and I don't want to spend extra hours learning a lot of lines every day. I have a family, a wife and kids and grandkids, so I come in without reading the daily script and spend some time setting everything up with the teleprompters. Believe me, it's a lot quicker this way."

So I tried his approach, hoping it might relieve me of all that memorization each day. But I just couldn't make it work well. The presence of the prompter, just off my line of sight, was disconcerting, and sensing it there broke my concentration and made me lose connection with my character.

Also, it seemed a bit dishonest to suggest you were portraying a character naturally when actually the portrayal was something you were reading rather than showing. I worked best when I knew my lines and had a bit of room to improvise around those lines. The teleprompter made that difficult to do.

A strange thing happened once I began to play Brent Davis. The dynamics of the show began to change. It had to do with the way I played the character. Instead of an unpleasant, of-fensive drunk, Brent Davis became likable. The audience began to empathize with him, to see his point of view. And strangely enough, the producers had trouble with that.

"You don't play him heavy enough," one of the producers complained to me.

"He's a father," I pointed out, "and he loves his daughter."

"He's also a drunk and a bum."

As we closed in on three months after I had joined the cast, I was called to a meeting in the production office. Behind the desk was the executive producer and off to the side was his assistant.

"We got a problem," the producer began, once I was seated. "Your character. He's too likable. We're getting letters, even phone calls."

"Positive audience reaction is good, isn't it?" It never hurt to emphasize what I had brought to the show.

"In this case, it's *not* good," the producer said, and I could see the assistant nodding in support. "Look, the script calls for this character to get killed off three months from now, but the way you're playing him, he becomes too popular to be killed off. You've made him too likable."

"And then what do we do?" added the assistant, who annoyed me by speaking at all.

Sadly, they already had their minds made up, and there wasn't anything I could do about it. The script had called for a drunken golf pro who made trouble for everyone, and that's the way the show was to be played. They informed me that they'd hired another actor who would take over my role, that my work on the show was finished after three months, rather than the six months in my original contract.

"We need to make sure this character comes off as a bum," the producer said, "and the guy we've hired looks and acts a hell of a lot more screwed up than you do. And that's the point, don't you see?"

Well, I did and I didn't, but there was no point beating the dead horse that was me.

I walked away from that encounter even less enthralled with the soaps than I had been. It wasn't just embarrassment at being replaced. It was the fact my acting ability was called into question, and that was a new and insulting experience for me, especially since the soaps were widely considered among the least challenging gigs an actor could find. If my acting could stumble with the soaps, what might happen when I was faced with more challenging roles? Indecision and concern swirled around my mind for weeks. Yet, somehow, through it all, I knew I was exaggerating things. Most actors, inevitably, suffered through down periods where they questioned their acting talent and their overall commitment to acting. On a certain level, the business demanded such personal interaction and judgment that there was no way everyone could be satisfied every time be each performance. Once you created a personal standard for achievement, it became one person's opinion against another's opinion, and sometimes the controlling opinion went against you.

So, I tucked my concerns away and decided that what had happened was a learning experience. When you take certain aspects of the acting life for granted--namely the certainties in a performance contract—you did so at your peril.

I've mentioned before that irony can play a large role in an actor's career. The nature of one's acting experiences is often a reprogramming of something that's been experienced before.

It might be a new and much less sympathetic twist on a role the actor played twenty years earlier.

Or it might be finding success in a role the actor had low expectations for when first cast or being directed by the ex-husband of his current wife or playing a real life character who is thoroughly detested by the actor. Sometimes, the one thing you'd promised yourself you would avoid becomes unavoidable.

And that's what happened with me and the soaps.

A few months after I walked away from *The Young and the Restless*, my agent, Morrie, called.

He told me that the producers at *Dallas* had been in touch. "They want to talk to you," he said.

Dallas. I recalled nine years earlier when they were first putting the show together, and the producers wanted me to read for the part of Ray Krebs, the illegitimate son of the Ewing family patriarch. The show was a major hit, year after year, a full hour of prime time weekly television. The actors were now household names.

And what had I done nine years earlier when I'd been approached about the Ray Krebs role? No, thanks, I'd said to the producers, not for me. I felt shame, remembering my disdain in those days. It was just episodic television, I felt, little more than a fancy soap opera, and where would the acting challenge come from? I was more interested in movie acting, and a nighttime soap opera just didn't carry the prestige or career enhancement I was looking for.

But nine years later, things were certainly different. It started with the salary.

"They're offering $5000 a show," Morrie said, and I let out a whistle. I was used to $750 a show when doing the standard soaps. "And the pressure's not the same," he added. This was a weekly show, and they took several days to shoot each episode.

The overall quality was better too, Morrie pointed out. The production team had been working together for years. The lighting and the sound were better. The sets were more elaborate and the episodes had more depth. The critics may have called it a soap opera, but Morrie insisted, "It's prime time television. The ratings are top of the scale and everybody's making really good money."

I asked myself a simple question: What's not to like here? My disgust for the soaps hadn't really changed, but most of the reasons I didn't like them didn't really apply with *Dallas*. I reminded myself in the television hierarchy, this was the top.

And I was there.

I was offered the role of U.S. Senator Andrew Dowling, who has an affair with Donna Culver Krebs, played by Susan Howard. It was a twist of fate. When first approached to join the cast of *Dallas*, nine years earlier, I was slated to play Ray Krebs, the ranch foreman, illegitimate son of the Ewing patriarch and Donna's television husband. Now, I played the lover of Krebs's wife, who moved to Washington to do lobbying work for the Ewing family. It was a meaty part, and it came with a bonus all working actors seek, a recurring role which allowed me to appear in numerous episodes, hopefully from season to season.

I never did have to read for the part, and from the moment I sat down with the producers to discuss the role, it seemed as if everything was already decided. It felt similar to what happened when I met Robert Redford to discuss *Downhill Racer*. What I didn't know until later was how I had been chosen. Since my character was going to play opposite Susan Howard's character, and the relationship between them would be intimate, the producers felt she should have a say in who was cast. Susan and her real life husband were given a stack of ten black and white head shots of prospective actors and told to choose any they found "interesting." They placed the photos on the floor and studied them closely. Gradually, they narrowed the field until my photo was the one they kept coming back to.

"So," Susan laughed as she told me, "the choice was unanimous. You were the one."

As it turned out, Susan was a delight to work with. She had a good actor's intuitive sense about portraying emotional level and intimacy. She knew when and how much to turn on and when to cut back. It's a skill not every actor possesses. After the first couple of episodes, I was feeling very good about my role, how I was playing it and how comfortable it was to work with Susan. But as I've mentioned elsewhere, an actor should never assume the future is already written. At best, an actor's life is an uneasy compromise between expectation and reality, where change can happen at any time.

And that's what happened in *Dallas*. Once, I saw how easily Susan and I worked together, I had hopes that we could play our roles into the indefinite future.

But it became clear that my role would slowly evaporate after several months, as Susan's character was to be written out of the show. I didn't know until weeks after I'd signed my contract that Susan and her husband were evangelical Christians, and they had been growing uncomfortable with the sexuality and immoral behavior being portrayed on the show. Susan had been on *Dallas* almost from the beginning, and as the story line grew less uplifting and more scandalous, she and her husband found it increasingly difficult to justify being there.

So, before I came on the show, they made a deal with the producers that she would be written out. To make that work, the producers decided her character would move alone to Washington, leave her husband behind and have an affair with my character. They would become a couple and slowly fade away from the story.

As it turned out, I appeared in 14 episodes of *Dallas*, usually wearing a tuxedo and frequently at a party. My character represented Texas in the Senate and was mostly supportive of what the Ewing Oil Company wanted to do. But I've often wondered where the show might have gone if Susan and I could have continued to play our roles into the show's ensuing years.

The *Dallas* set was friendly and relaxed, and the cast intermingled easily. Larry Hagman played JR, one of the leads, and his mother was Mary Martin who had played Peter Pan on Broadway for years. Larry and I chatted frequently off set, and one time, I mentioned that Helene, when she was only ten years old, had seen Mary Martin perform the role of and went home, climbed on the piano and tried to fly away, just as she'd seen Peter Pan do a few hours earlier.

Helene ended up with a broken ankle.

"Do you have a recording of the show?" he asked.

We did and I brought it in to show him.

"Mind if I take this for a few days?"

I shrugged. I could always buy another.

A couple of weeks later, he handed the recording back to me with an inscription: "To Helene. Stay off the piano! Signed, Mary Martin."

Chapter Eleven

Featured Player

As an actor climbs the rungs of career success, the highest rung, of course, is stardom. A laudatory goal, to be sure, but the reality is that only a few reach this level. Yet for most who fall short, there are other compensations.

Waiting for something like a huge break to happen is like betting you are going to get an inside straight in poker. It's possible but rarely successful. As the early years went along and my quest for stardom never quite materialized, I began to find pleasure in what I had accomplished, like as working with Robert Redford in *Downhill Racer* and James Stewart in *Shenandoah*.

Those were hardly starring roles, of course, but they exposed me to talented people from whom I learned a great deal.

At the very least, I found myself assuming a more professional, less wide-eyed acceptance of what it really took to make a successful movie. I had developed acting skills that allowed me to understand when and why a performance worked. I had become a professional, consistent in my performances and clear about what it took to bring out my strongest portrayal.

The rung directly below star is the featured player level, and it is where compensation for missing stardom can be attained for so many.

One day in 1974, I got a call from my agent. "Fox is casting for a television movie and they want to talk to you." It turned out the movie was *Stowaway to the Moon,* based on a book of the same name by William Roy Shelton. We were only five years from the Apollo moon landings when Neil Armstrong and Buzz Aldrin electrified the world. Interest in the moon and space exploration had not wound down since that time. The film injected watchable characters and made it a heart-warming yet suspenseful adventure.

When I got to the Fox studios and met the casting people, it almost seemed as if the role was waiting for me. The director was Andy McLaglen, son of the famed Hollywood character actor and Academy Award winner, Victor McLaglen.

One of the first things the casting director said to me was, "Andy's looking forward to working with you, again." I remembered Andy from *Shenandoah,* which he had also directed. I considered him one of the finest people I ever worked with. Empathetic, careful and low-key, he had Hollywood blood in his veins, and making movies was natural to him.

The story was based on the recently concluded Apollo mission to the moon. But in the movie an eleven-year-old boy, played by Michael Link, was able to stow away on the space craft and suddenly appeared as the ship went beyond earth's orbit, headed toward the moon. The boy lived near Cape Canaveral and was fascinated by space flight. His father worked at the space facility and the boy hung around a lot, so his presence near the launch site didn't create undue suspicion. The night before launch, he sneaked aboard and hid in the garbage storage section, which would be one of the last places prior to launch that anyone might search.

I played the part of Pelham, commander of the lunar module that orbited the moon while my two astronaut companions, played by Jeremy Slate and Morgan Paull, were on the ground.

Back at mission control, the overall commander was Lloyd Bridges. From the moment the kid appeared, the crew knew we had to keep his presence unknown. Otherwise, the mission would likely be aborted.

So, we talked to the kid and were impressed by how much he knew about space travel and how interested he was in what we were doing. Our feelings for him grew quite strong as we closed in on the moon, and soon, were in orbit around it. The other two crew members climbed into the lunar landing vehicle and headed for the surface while the kid and me maintained a continual moon orbit.

Then, disaster struck. With my companions on the lunar surface, suddenly I got violently ill, choking on my own vomit. I was wearing an air-tight space helmet, and if something didn't happen really fast, I was going to drown and the entire mission would become a catastrophe.

But the kid came to the rescue. While I was choking, he found a vacuum hose and cleaner, attached it to my equipment and gradually, the space inside my helmet was cleaned up and I was able to breathe again. The kid had saved my life.

In gratitude, I offered to show him how to fly the lunar module, which he accepted gratefully. The learning process was surprisingly short because he'd already stored so much knowledge about space travel in his head. He was able to fly the space vehicle part of the way back to Earth and became the real hero of the drama.

While the drama portrayed us in space throughout, the actual shooting was done mostly in the studio. We had to make it seem as if we were in space, so we had to act as if we were weightless. Sometimes, that was difficult, even though it was also fun.

Back in those days, we didn't have the luxury of the modern special effects we have now, when an entire body can be seen as weightlessness via green screen. You made up for the limitations of effects by hinting at total weightlessness, showing your arms moving in slow motion, for example, so it appeared as if you were floating. We walked very slowly and deliberately. At first this was difficult, especially since you had to be aware of how every aspect of your body appeared And all the while, concentrating on movement, you had to remember your lines. It did get easier the more we did it, but I would never say I was relaxed while portraying the character.

From the standpoint authenticity, one fact did stand out for me. On the second day of shooting, I wore my space suit, my costume, and I noticed something stamped boldly on the inside of the collar: "SCHWEICKART R." There was nothing else, no number, no symbol, just a name. We'd heard rumors that 20th Century Fox had been able to obtain some vintage space travel equipment for the movie. I wondered whether this also applied to the costuming. Fortunately, we had several advisers from NASA on set. Space travel was still so new and uncertain that the producers didn't want to destroy the movie's authenticity with a major error.

So I showed my costume to one of these advisers. He shook it out, examined the stamp inside the collar, checked it for size and said, "This is what they wore on Apollo Nine six years ago." he said. Then, he added "The suits are lighter now, more durable."

"And the name?"

"Yes, that's his."

Rusty Schweickart, the third man on the Apollo Nine mission, the lunar module pilot and a New Jersey guy. He'd been to the moon, and I had the honor of wearing his space suit.

A few days, later I wrote to him and told him about the movie and that I would be wearing his space suit. I thought he'd want to know. Sure enough, not long afterwards, I received a note from him thanking me for getting in touch and saying how pleased he was his actual space suit would be used. He wished us well, and when I shared his note with the rest of the cast, there were broad smiles all around.

A couple of years later, another featured player role came my way, only this time it was in a made-for-television-movie which appeared on ABC, called *She Dressed to Kill*. The main story involved a fashion show at an elegant, mountain-top French chateau, where the fashion models began to die, and no one could quite figure it out. I played Michael Barton who, with his ex-wife, played by Jessica Walter, had owned the modeling agency that was putting on the fashion show. However, not long before the show opens, Michael's ex-wife stole control of the agency from him. He has vowed to destroy her. After he slipped onto the chateau grounds, he started killing the fashion models, one-by-one. The police were called and a sheriff named Halsey showed up to conduct the murder investigation. However, Halsey actually was my character, Michael Barton, in disguise.

It was the first time I played more than a single character in the same production. The transition back and forth between the characters was difficult at first, because they were such different personalities. But the further along the production went, the easier it became.

One thing did bother me about the Sheriff Halsey character, though. They fitted me with a disguise, but I just didn't think it was effective enough. I wore a phony nose, some thick, horn-rimmed glasses and a cowboy hat and that was it.

"Wouldn't it work better if I wore a complete rubber face mask?" I asked one of the producers. "Then, no one could possibly recognize it was me."

The producer wasn't convinced. "Relax," he said. "The audience will never figure it out."

What about audience reaction when I become unmasked, I wondered?

"Wouldn't it make more impact if I whip off a full mask than just a phony nose and some glasses?"

"Believe me," he responded, "we know our audiences pretty well." And that was that.

Connie Sellecca played one of the leads, a model who finally discovered my real identity, and in the final scene, we were on a gondola moving up the mountain towards the chateau. We actually shot this scene in Palm Springs on the well-known tourist gondola.

At that point in the story, she had figured things out. She confronted me and when I made a move towards her, as the tram reaches its highest point, she stepped out of the way and pushed me off so I fell to my death. What gave the scene a particular power was that when she pushed me, in the background was the actual wheel of the tram turning, turning, as the tram car glides to a stop.

As I've mentioned, when you're cast in a made-for-television movie, you expect a much shorter production schedule than if you've been cast in a feature film. Often, with the former, you can measure your total time on set in days, while with the latter, it's usually measured in weeks.

For example, with the television movie, *She's Dressed to Kill*, and even as a featured player, I was on set only 14 days. Now, contrast that with my work a couple of years later on a feature film. The production took more than seven weeks to complete, and you begin to understand why an actor yearns for the feature film route. Not only is the compensation better, but so is the overall production, the script and the directing because there's time to get things done the right way.

The inexorable demands of time and scheduling in television work force actors and production staff into compromises that aren't as present in the feature film world, and that usually makes for stronger work, In 1986, my agent got me cast in an independent film that starred Charles Bronson and his wife, Jill Ireland, directed by Peter Hunt, an elegant British theater pro who made a name for himself directing several James Bond films. The story concerned a Secret Service agent, Bronson, assigned to protect the First Lady of the United States from assassination.

It was replete with cross-country chases, violence and political drama. I played "Zipper," one of the Secret Service agents working with Bronson's character. As it turned out, Bronson and I shared a great deal of screen time. Most of my screen appearances in the movie were alongside him.

The original title was *My Affair with the President's Wife*, based on the book of the same name by Richard Sale. But the producers thought that might be insulting to the Presidency, so they changed it to *The President's Wife*. But then, someone mentioned the story was more about an assassination than who the President's wife was. Charles Bronson weighed in as well, telling an interviewer that a movie about a wife "...is not what people expect from one of my pictures."

So yet another change was made. This time it was simply called *The Assassin*. But apparently that was no good, because another producer complained that the new title had a negative connotation and might freak out the Washington establishment, whose cooperation and professional input was needed. Finally, they decided on *Assassination*, which to me doesn't sound a lot more positive than *The Assassin*. Bronson grudgingly admitted that yes, "There's an assassination involved," and they decided to leave it at that.

Three years before, Jill Ireland had been operated on for breast cancer, and she'd been struggling with the disease. What none of us knew until well into production was that Charles Bronson had conceived of doing the movie as a memorial to his wife, regardless of her cancer prognosis. And so he was deeply involved, emotionally and physically, in how things worked out. He arranged it so she would play the lead, as the President's wife. None of us was aware of her fragile physical condition during production. In fact, Jill Ireland herself, seemed confident about being able to do the work, saying to a reporter that being cast in this role, "...validates the fact I'm working, feeling good, looking good and able to spend long hours on the set."

Sadly, less than three years after we finished production on this movie, the cancer returned and the brave and lovely Jill Ireland passed away.

Working with Charles Bronson was not always a pleasant experience. He was a secretive man, not particularly approachable or friendly, though I wondered from time to time whether his stand-offishness had something to do with his contained grief over his wife's physical condition.

He never mentioned it, of course, and both he and Jill Ireland maintained a firm, professional attitude on set, never discussing personal issues.

Every morning you arrived on set, there would be Bronson in his chair, and the most you'd get would be a grunted "Hello" or a nod, never anything more. Later, when I worked with him, he'd be polite but he'd get right in there and do his job. There was never any small talk, anything that wasn't script related conversation. It became obvious he didn't want to develop any personal relationships on set.

Not so with Jill, who was friendly and excited about her role and the movie. One day, Jill and I were sitting around between takes, and I noticed a young actor across from us who had a small part in the film. Jill told me his name was Paul, so I asked him where he was from, how long he'd been acting, where had he worked. Jill piped up that he was her son by a prior marriage to actor David McCallum.

"I've wanted to work with him for years," she smiled.

How I would have loved to work with either of my sons. I was about to ask Paul how he enjoyed working with his mother, when I felt a presence behind us and I turned. There was Bronson, leaning against a wall, in earshot of what we had been saying. Bronson gave Jill a hard look, and said with biting sarcasm, "Why don't you tell him your whole life?"

I felt a chill down my back. "Mister Bronson," I said hurriedly, since he wasn't the kind of person you called by his first name. "I'm sorry, I wasn't trying to pry."

Jill held up a hand for me to stop. "Oh, Charlie," she laughed, "it's not a big deal."

"Right," he grunted and walked off the set.

My featured player status continued to develop and a year later, my agent was able to get me cast in a sitcom, something that after almost thirty years as an actor I'd never tried. You could call sitcoms "cousins" to the soaps, in that there's a constant and steady regular cast with an occasional guest artist, a regular performance schedule and the basic setting is the same show after show. What's different, of course, is that the time demands are not as stringent on the sitcoms.

You have a week to learn lines instead of overnight, and that means the performances and characterizations can be more developed. Sitcoms use the same lead characters each show, while with the soaps, the lead characters are more numerous and shift over each episode..

And then there is the production itself. Sitcoms are often performed before a live audience, while that never happens with the soaps. For me, working with a live audience in television was a new experience and a bit scary. Up to now, all my television work had been in the studio with only the crew, the cast and the control room people as an audience. With the sitcom, there would be actual human beings sitting out there, all strangers to me.

There were four large television cameras you had to be aware of because they were in constant motion. The last thing you wanted to do was to trip over one them with that live audience out there watching you fall on your face.

The sitcom was *Nine to Five* and it had been running for several years before I joined the cast. It blossomed out of a 1980 movie of the same name that starred Dolly Parton. The television spin-off followed the original story line fairly closely. It was set in an office where the women workers banded together and rebelled against the male workers who exploited them and put them down for years. The women, in both the movie and on the television screen, showed themselves as smarter and more astute than the men and ended up setting the agenda for everyone.

I played Sherman Oaks, an inveterate womanizer, who was called a "serial seducer" in the script. The object of my affection was Sally Struthers, one of the show's stars and formerly a featured player on Norman Lear's ground-breaking 1970s sitcom, *All in the Family*. Sally played a secretary in *Nine to Five*, and we met at a training session for emergency medical personnel.

We strongly connected and she invited me back to her apartment, which she shared with two others. But neither were home when we got there, so we made for her bedroom, closed the door and engaged in noisy sex. But we heard the front door open and one of her roommates returned.

Sally hushed me, told me to stay where I was and slipped out of the bedroom to alert her roommate so she wouldn't walk in on us.

But my character, Sherman Oaks, the serial seducer, saw only opportunity. I remained on the bed, shouting through the ajar door, "Come on in. Let's get together!"

The cameras switched to Sally and her roommate discussing what to do. In a few moments, they decided to take the plunge and opened the bedroom door, only to find me stretched out, dead of a heart attack. The rest of the show, then, was devoted to getting rid of my body.

And, of course, there were humorous stops and starts before they succeeded.

During my first day on the set, I walked into my dressing room and there were some flowers and a note from Sally Struthers.

"Dear Jim," she wrote, "I want you to know I've never kissed anyone in this show yet, so please be gentle." The script did call for me to kiss her as part of the seduction scene. So, I tried to do as she asked. And that seemed to bond us. We blended our roles seamlessly, as if we'd been working together for years. She was fun to work with, and after a single take, I began to anticipate where she would move and how I should move with her. And as for the studio audience, Sally set the tone. We slid into our roles so well that within twenty minutes, the live audience was just not a factor.

Sometimes, working as a featured player doesn't mean you're around until the end of the film or show. Look at *Nine to Five*, where I was killed off part way through, and a major part of the story still had not unraveled. You're a featured player if your role has a major impact on the overall story. Even though my character expired, his already dead presence drove the story forward.

It's easier, of course, to argue for featured player status when your role runs throughout most of the movie, and that's what happened with *Judicial Consent*, a 1994 independent courtroom thriller, that starred Bonnie Bedelia and Dabney Coleman. After more than three decades in front of the cameras, I'd acquired a status for doing older man roles. That's what came my way in *Judicial Consent*. I played Trenton Clarkson, a state prosecutor, who tried to convict a young man of murder. It turned out the victim was a close, personal friend of the trial judge, played by Bonnie Bedelia. But Bonnie's character had a few secrets she was not sharing. One of them was that she was in a loveless marriage. In the opening scenes, she was portrayed having steamy sex with a young law clerk.

Then, the victim turned up dead, a suspect was arrested and Bonnie Bedelia's character was assigned as the trial judge. Rumors started to fly, including the fact the judge and the victim not only knew one another well but had an affair. Suddenly, the judge had some explaining to do I was the character assigned to prosecute the case, and from my earliest appearance on set, I felt comfortable in the role. The set, itself, helped me. We filmed on location in Dearborn, Michigan, in a well-constructed, classic courthouse that reeked of tradition and substance. It had deep, dark wood, gleaming brass fittings, high ceilings, polished mahogany benches, the type of courtroom you'd expect Clarence Darrow to excel in.

What I liked about my role was how I controlled what happened on the screen, how I was the aggressor and others had to contend with and, sometimes, even appease that aggression. In screenwriter language, my character was a "story mover," someone who pushed things along and influenced who did what to whom and when. I enjoyed playing the role so much that when we weren't filming or rehearsing, I thought of my role in relation to Perry Mason, the fictional Erle Stanley Gardner lawyer-sleuth. It was so satisfying to find clues or come up with ideas that would solve a major crime and convict the crafty, slippery perpetrator. One of the joys of the acting life is playing a character you would have loved being in another lifetime.

Chapter Twelve

Actors As Artists

It was a gorgeous day for a celebration, a soft, tender breeze out of a crystalline blue sky with a high sun. There we were, confident stars of our own production.

It was 1992, and it was publication day. Our book, *Actors as Artists*, was available officially.

My coauthor, Dick Gautier, and I inhaled the scene: a chic Beverly Hills restaurant, A-list actors, assorted film industry movers, large profile cut-outs of Dick and me, ample food and drink and several stacks of our book available for purchase and signing by us.

Gene Hackman, whose art and profile were in the book, and with whom I had acted decades earlier on *Downhill Racer*, took charge.

"Everybody!" he called out. "Let's give the authors a round of applause for recognizing actors can have great talent beyond their acting."

An exuberant wave of applause swept across us. My mind went back more than three decades to the set of the Civil War drama, *Shenandoah*. That was where I had the first glimmer of an idea for *Actors as Artists*. On the set, Jimmy Stewart and I bonded over chess. Our almost daily interaction created an easy familiarity that moved beyond the movie we were working on.

We talked about our mutual interest in architecture, how we had studied it in college, and he added he knew other actors who had studied architecture and painted.

It turned out that painting had acquired a sophisticated cachet with the Hollywood establishment in the early 1960s. Actors vied to project themselves as multitalented artists, rather than one-dimensional screen personalities. Many of them were in contact and took classes with Sergei Bongart, a Russian émigré-painter whose work eventually, years later, was featured in numerous museums around the country. Bongart had emigrated to America in the late 1940s, having studied art in Kiev, Prague, Vienna and Munich. He opened an art school in Los Angeles, and gradually the Hollywood elite discovered him, impressed with his emphasis on dramatic coloring and his empathetic, rustic depictions of his early life in Russia. He offered continental flair as well as highly skilled grounding in oil and watercolors. By the early 1960s, he could boast a loyal following of Hollywood actors and actresses who saw him as their painting mentor.

On the set of *Shenandoah*, I pondered Jimmy Stewart's words, when he said, "As a matter of fact, my wife is having her portrait painted *at this very moment* by Claudette Colbert."

An idea began to take shape. Hollywood actors and artists, could be shown crossing over.

Could there be a book there? Could I write it? Could I find enough actors who were also artists?

Even more to the point was whether I *should* write it. After all, writing wasn't what I did.

I was an actor, and that was where my attention had to be focused.

Reluctantly, I pushed the idea of a book on acting and artists to the back of mind and redoubled my efforts to be the best actor

I could be. But as my acting career moved forward, and the years sped by, I never really forgot about the idea of the book.

Every once in a while, unexpectedly, the thought of acting and artists tickled my mind.

Then, I wondered if anyone has done a book on the subject. I worried whether there were enough actors who actually painted. And would anyone else think it was a good idea? I'd look at my image in the mirror and realized that as I posing those questions, I was really talking about myself, as an actor and painter. If I was doing those things, wouldn't other actors too?

But that was about as far as I'd go with the idea because of the obligation to make a living and support my family. And off I'd go to another audition or a production meeting for an upcoming movie or television show or a meeting with my agent, and the book itch would subside.

For twenty-five years or so, I carried the idea for a book on actors and painting tucked away in the furthest reaches of my mind, barely aware it was there.

Then, one day in 1990, my agent called. "I got you a gig doing a commercial," he said, naming the production company that would be putting it together. "They want you at the studio tomorrow."

He added that the commercial was for the Mars Candy Company, which made the wellknown Mars Bar.

"I'm not a candy lover," I said.

"But you'll do the commercial?"

Pick your fights, I thought to myself. "Sure," I said, "I'll be there."

It was a typical commercial shoot. There were lots of unfamiliar faces. The sponsor's people huddled with the director. A couple of ad agency representatives read over the script. Boxes of the sponsor's product were piled in a corner, and the actors sat by themselves, scripts in hand, waiting and watching.

"Welcome!" said a voice from the middle of the sitting actors. "You one of us?"

The voice came from a nice-looking young man with a mop of black hair and a bemused expression.

I nodded slowly. "Looks like it," I said.

He stood up and held out his hand. "Dick Gautier," he said, and he pointed to an empty seat. "They'll be calling us shortly."

While we waited, Dick Gautier and I compared our scripts and the roles we would be playing. We each had lines and full body close-ups, so we could claim to be featured on the commercial.

I noticed he had done a line drawing on the back of a script page. At first, I thought it was just doodling, something to make the waiting go faster. But after we sat down, he started adding to the drawing, and I could see the outline of a face, which seemed to resemble the commercial's director, whom I had met earlier. But there was something odd about the drawing. It showed a squinty eye and a fang-like tooth, and that look wasn't present on the face of the director I had met.

Gautier caught me looking at his drawing and smiled. "He's known as 'old adhesive tape,' tighter than hell with money and budgets. Sponsors and producers love him. Actors? Not so much."

"Better not let him see it," I said.

Gautier folded the drawing and put it away. "Got lots of these," he added.

I was intrigued. Here was someone looking to play a role in a television commercial who also created line drawings, and they were *good* line drawings, too. That old idea about actors and artists crept into the front of my mind. "But you're really an actor, right?"

"I guess you could say that," he said. But Gautier went on to explain that he'd started out as a nightclub comic and singer in the late 1950s. The acting followed because in 1960, he played the lead in the Broadway production of *Bye Bye Birdie* and received a Tony nomination.

That produced roles for him in various television sitcoms through the 1960s and 1970s and into the 1980s, including as Hymie the robot in the popular series, *Get Smart*. During that time, he was also a frequent panelist on game shows such as *The Match Game* and *Family Feud*.

But he was also indulging his other passion, which was drawing, especially cartoons and caricatures. But when he and I met, the drawings were generally circulated only among his friends, and none had been published.

"You act and draw," I said, mentioning I was sure there were other actors who did the same thing just as with painting. "In fact," I added, "I've been toting around in my mind a book idea for the last twenty-five years, where I interview actors who are also painters, sculptors, that type of thing."

His reaction was instantaneous. "What a great idea!" he exclaimed. "I love it!" And he reeled off a couple of actors he knew who painted, including Peter Falk, star of the *Colombo* detective series and Candice Bergen, who was getting rave reviews on her sitcom, *Murphy Brown*.

He also had a connection to the Henry Fonda estate and he knew that Fonda, who had died a few years earlier, had loved to paint. That spurred my energy about the project. For the first time since I had talked with Jimmy Stewart, I felt it could truly be done. I thought of my *Downhill Racer* pals. Robert Redford, I knew, had attended Pratt Institute in New York. Suddenly, Dick Gautier and I were trading names of actor-artists and barely able to contain our growing enthusiasm for the idea.

I said, almost shouting, "Okay, let's do it!"

I remember Dick nodded vigorously, a big smile on his face.

And then, the smile disappeared, and his face grew somber. Dick's next words came slowly. "What exactly does 'it' mean, here?"

Neither of us had more than a vague idea at this point, though we knew we had something worthwhile to work on. Neither of us had ever written a book, nor did we think of ourselves as any kind of writers. But we sensed we were on to an idea which would intrigue a lot of 158 people: The names were familiar and we would show a side of these well-known people which had rarely surfaced.

"And," Dick added, "because these people are really artists, whether they're acting or painting."

I said amen to that.

We decided I'd contact Redford and Hackman and see what kind of reaction I'd get to the idea of showing their painting talents publicly. We fashioned a simple question for them: "Would you like to be in a book that highlights your painting alongside your bio?" We figured the biography was necessary to provide context for the art work, so the reader would be able to tie them both together.

Within days, we heard back from both Redford and Hackman, agreeing to participate. So, we expanded our efforts and within a week, we'd heard from the Henry Fonda estate. Their reply was, "We'd really like to be involved."

Then Peter Falk jumped aboard, and suddenly, we felt the thrilling momentum and an evolving book idea.

We began setting up interviews with various actors and made appointments to photograph their art. We structured the interviews to be as straightforward as possible. Dick and I wanted to avoid any hint of artistic criticism or preference. We asked them why they painted, what types of paintings they liked to do, which surfaces they liked to work with, how they learned about their craft and who had helped the along the way.

Over the next several months, we devoted ourselves to the interviews and to photography. In the meantime, the crucial question of what to do with the eventual manuscript was pushed to the side. Finally, though, we amassed all the material we needed and it was time to try and market the manuscript.

But how? With whom?

Then, by chance, my agent mentioned he'd be attending the annual American Booksellers Association convention. It was held that year in nearby Anaheim in about a week. One of the actors he represented had written a memoir, and he wanted to see what interest there might be in such a book.

"It's the largest gathering of booksellers, agents, publishers and other book people every year," he said, estimating the crowd to be well over 20,000 for the four day convention, "Some writers attend, as well," he added.

That got me thinking. What if I went and tried to find someone who might be interested in publishing what Dick Gautier and I had been putting together?

I ran the idea by Dick and he thought it was worth a try.

"Who knows," he said, "we could strike gold."

So I put together a portfolio of half a dozen actor-artists, which included their paintings and their bios. I bought a ticket and walked through the door of what is colloquially known as the "ABA."

And I realized within minutes that this type of convention wasn't designed for writers to pitch book ideas. The space was enormous, a convention center with an extremely high ceiling and bustling crowds. Numerous booths were placed along a grid of aisles and pathways featuring all aspects of the book publishing and selling business. There was not a quiet corner to be had, a space where one could curl up with a book. Clearly, this was a place where booksellers and publishers met and made deals with one another. The language spoken at the ABA was commercial, not literary.

But I was there, I'd paid for a ticket and I had a book concept to sell.

It couldn't have been more than five minutes after I walked through the door and started down one of the teeming aisles that I spotted a booth with the prominent sign, "Salem House Publishers." On top of a makeshift counter was a pile of books and behind the counter was a middle-aged man casually observing the passing crowds. I looked at him, he looked at me, and I thought. I might as well. There's no reason to wait.

He held out his hand. "Peter Ackroyd," he said, with a smile.

I shook his hand, introduced myself, then took a deep breath and pulled out the sample portfolio I'd created.

"What do you think about this?" I asked, simply.

As he read it over, I watched his facial expression become more and more engaged. He turned to me and grinned. "You believe in serendipity?"

I wasn't quite sure what he meant, but he tapped the portfolio with his finger and added, "I really like this."

It turned out that Salem House was owned by a titan of the media business, none other than, Rupert Murdoch. Peter Ackroyd was an Australian publisher who had been recruited specifically to join Salem House and develop a line of art books.

And it was apparent that what I was offering fit right in.

The day we met was Peter's first day at the book convention, and in fact, I was one of the first people to stop by his booth. He tapped the portfolio again. "This is good, and I'd like to share it with my colleagues. How about leaving it with me for a couple of hours?"

My first reaction was pleasure and excitement. Who would have predicted that something like this could happen within minutes of walking through the door? For an instant, I felt the heady swirl of success. I thought of Dick Gautier and me as published writers, with our names on the cover.

But suddenly, I had a queasy feeling. I wondered whether things were happening too fast.

Could it be this easy? I took a deep breath and knew I had to be more patient because if something was this easy, it was usually *too* easy.

Reluctantly, I reached for the portfolio. I thanked him for his comments and let him know how excited I felt.

But I said, "Let me come back to you later today after I've shown this to a few other people."

Disappointment clouded his face but he nodded. "Just make sure you come back here before you leave tonight."

I spent the next several hours pushing my way through the crowded aisles, stopping when I spotted a publisher's booth that seemed a good target for our book. But I wasn't able to spark the kind of interest in our book idea that Peter Ackroyd had shown. At best, the publisher representatives offered lukewarm interest in a book about actors as artists. A couple even had the nerve to say outright that it would never sell.

So, after chiding myself for doubting Peter Ackroyd, I wandered back to the Salem House booth. When Peter saw me, his face lit up. I handed him back the portfolio. I told him, "You said you liked it."

"I did and I do," he responded. "I really do."

A week later, Peter called with the formal contract offer: a $40,000 advance against royalties, split between Dick Gautier and me, and publication of the book no later than a year after we turned in the manuscript.

After Dick and I took a couple of days to get over the shock of such a sizable advance, we signed the contract.

Peter's words echoed in our ears. "Okay time to get to work now."

And so we started putting the book together, setting up interviews and photographing art work. Our original contacts suggested other people and soon we had a list of 30, then 40, then 50 people to get in touch with as potential subjects for the book. Major stars of the past and present appeared on our list. They included icons like Lionel Barrymore, Jimmy Cagney, Van Johnson, Kim Novak and Jane Seymour.

Soon, more than six months had gone by, and as our file of interviews and photos grew more voluminous, so did our enthusiasm.

Then, one day, Peter Ackroyd called and his voice was somber. "Guess what?" he said then came right to the point, giving us the bad news. "Rupert Murdoch has sold Salem House Books, and the new owners have no interest in publishing art books."

Just like that, our dream was gone. We were back where we started. We had a good idea for a book but nowhere to publish it.

Peter went on, breaking the stunned silence. "Since we, Salem House, own the rights to publishing your book, and the new owners have no interest in acquiring those rights, we've decided to give those rights back to you and Dick."

My head was spinning. The first question that came out of my mouth was, "What about the $40,000 advance?" I hadn't spent all of my share but certainly, some of it was gone. Would we have to give that back?

Suddenly, my mood changed dramatically. Peter said six words that both amazed and relieved my mind. He replied, "You guys can keep that advance."

So, we had the book back again. Yet both of us felt unsettled and dissatisfied. True, we were richer, but we didn't have a published book.

For the next few months, we struggled to sell the book elsewhere, but we met the same lukewarm reaction from other publishers that I had encountered at the ABA convention.

"…Interesting but too expensive to produce."

"…A bunch of amateur painters and sculptors trading on their famous names."

"Who'd actually *buy* this book?"

We kept hoping we'd meet another Peter Ackroyd. But the more people we spoke to, the more we sensed he was one of a kind.

And our enthusiasm for the overall project began to flag. We began to wonder whether we shouldn't just put the book idea away and appreciate the fact that we got paid for a nonexistent book.

We had to forget being published writers, showing fine visual art from actors and surprising people, showing that their talents transcended what they did before the camera or on stage.

One day, after months of no movement on the book, Peter Ackroyd called. There was enthusiasm in his voice. "You guys have been on my mind," he said. "I'm back on the art book beat with a new publisher. What's the status of your *Actors as Artists* book?"

And with those few words, our spirits soared. I told him we still hadn't sold it, but still wanted to do so.

"Well," he said, letting a couple of seconds pass, "suppose I said we might be interested in publishing it. How would that strike you?"

"We'd love it," I said, knowing I was speaking for Dick, as well.

It turned out Peter had become a senior editor at Charles Tuttle Company, a small but respected New England publisher, and an art books list was what he'd been hired to develop. "I still really like your book concept," he said, "and I think there's a wider audience out there than many realize."

Then, he brought up money. "I remember how much Salem House had paid you, and I don't think we can do the same thing here. After all, you guys walked away with a bundle, and no one has a book to show for it." He added he wasn't resentful about our earlier advance but was unable to match it again.

"How about we settle on an advance against royalties of $10,000?" he suggested. "That'll show you we have solid interest in your book. And I can also go back to the boss and say we didn't break the bank in the deal."

That seemed fair to me, and Dick concurred after I spelled the details out to him.

"Guess it's time to get back to work," he said, and we signed the book contract a couple of days later.

We still had a bunch of interviews to do because we'd done very little after Salem House had pulled out of the contract. One meeting that sticks vividly in my mind is the day we went to Peter Falk's house. Dick had been friends with him for years and knew that Falk often did nude charcoal drawings in the privacy of his studio.

We brought along a photographer and walked in as Falk was at work at the easel, his nude model posed and motionless. We interviewed him while he continued to work. But after an hour, he called a break and stepped away from his easel while the model slipped into her robe.

Falk glanced out the studio window towards his house.

"Uh-oh," he said softly, noting his wife was on her way to the studio. Then, to the model, he grinned and remarked, "You better take your robe off. Otherwise, my wife will suspect something's been going on."

Later, after we'd finished the interview and the photos, he invited us up to his house for a drink. As we walked across the lawn, we heard a large tour bus stopping out front.

"Here's the home of Peter Falk," blared a voice through a loudspeaker. "He plays that wonderful detective Colombo on television..."

Falk turned and shooed us back toward the studio. "Oh crap," he grimaced. "Let's hide."

Our search for artists throughout the Hollywood acting community occasionally brought a surprising response. One was from Katherine Hepburn who painted but rarely showed her work. We got in touch with her and explained what we were doing.

It was a worthwhile project, she admitted. "But no, I don't want to be involved."

I was about to move on but Dick said, "Let's try it a different way." He suggested we write to her, rather than calling again, and list some of those who had already been interviewed, names like Edward G. Robinson and Robert Redford.

We got a noncommittal response from her. She thanked us for the invitation and did not reject us outright. The door was left open for further contact. So, we wrote her back, providing additional names of those who would be participating but we avoided putting any direct pressure on her to join us.

Finally, after five letters from us, each adding to our list of featured artists, she relented.

And one day, a package arrived from her. Inside was a beautiful still-life of a delicate, spindly, wooden chair. Titled simply "A Chair, oil," the chair in the painting was highlighted by colorful wall hangings of a lighthouse and a woman in a *Belle Epoque* dress and flowered hat.

In all, we interviewed 77 artists for the book. The great majority of them were painters, along with a few sculptors. Most of those we interviewed said that doing their art was a way to relax, to provide a departure from the collaborative effort of working with other actors, directors and producers. They just wanted some quiet time and a way to express themselves individually and not have to face a barrage of criticism or judgment. They were creating their art for themselves, and they intended to be their own singular audience.

"But art," as Dick and I wrote in the introduction to the book, "is not to be compared. It fails or succeeds on its own merits." Allowing those marvelous performers to show the world their visual creativity was one of the most enjoyable creative acts in my career. And the difficulty in accomplishing it made it even more memorable for me.

Chapter Thirteen

Commercials? Well, why Not?

IT WAS A strange sight. The late afternoon sun peeked over multicolored rooftops, illuminating an outdoor basketball court in the heart of Los Angeles' urban sprawl. Four men, at the foul line, played a basketball elimination game, until only one shooter remained. The banter was fierce, and it was obvious the players had had this competition before.

One of them, the most vocal and athletic looking, pointed to one of the others and shouted, "No way you're going to make that!"

I'm no basketball player, but what I witnessed was a group of television professionals on break who discovered a nearby basketball court and threw themselves into the competition, at least for the next few minutes. The loudest player was also the director of the television project, Joe Pytka, on his way to legendary status as the director-king of sports commercials. The other players were members of his crew, his cameraman, sound technician and assistant producer.

I'd been warned that this could happen by my agent. "You'll be working with Joe Pytka," he said. "The guy loves basketball. He'll work up a game on break."

And so he did. But I wasn't there for basketball. I'd been cast in the television project that Joe Pytka was to direct, a Nike sports commercial. For me, this was a new career move; I'd spent my early acting days focusing on movies and television drama. But by the 1970s, it was clear that doing commercials could provide a plus to the bread and butter scenario that every actor needs.

Doing commercials had a couple of drawbacks, of course. Your screen time was limited to 30 seconds, if that. Your upfront payday wasn't hefty. The essence of your role was to sell, to encourage viewers to buy the product. You didn't have pretensions that some artistic statement was being made.

"You want art," a wizened old director told me once. "Go to the museum." And he was right. An actor shouldn't kid him-or herself that what they were doing was more than it actually was. If we're pitching someone's laundry soap, it doesn't matter how you dress it up, it's still laundry soap.

The first thing I learned about doing commercials was getting cast in them doesn't arrive on your doorstep by chance. An actor needs an agent, but in this case not just any kind of agent.

What's needed is a commercial agent, someone who specializes in placing actors in this type of production. It's a specialization within the general agenting world, requiring a form of expertise that separates commercial agents from the broader category of general talent agents.

Actually, my entry into this world was more by accident than by design. It was the early 1970s, and I was trying to build a career. It was after my work in *Downhill Racer*, and my appearance in the television movie *Pursuit*, based on the Michael Crichton novel, *Binary*. One evening, the phone rang and a pleasant female voice asked to speak to me:

"This is Sonjia Warren Brandon," she said, "I just saw you on the Michael Crichton television movie, and I'd like to talk to you about doing some work for us."

"Us," it turned out was Commercials Unlimited, a Beverly Hills agency that specialized in placing actors in radio and television commercials. By the time she contacted me, Sonjia Brandon was on her way to becoming a legend in the commercials business, though it was still fairly early in her career.

We met for lunch a couple of days later. In the interim, I did a bit of homework, finding she was well-respected, experienced and someone who worked hard for her clients. When she called and identified herself, I admitted it was the first time I had heard her name. When she explained briefly why she was calling, I further admitted I'd never thought about using a special agent for getting work in commercials.

At lunch, though, she made it a lot clearer. At the time, she was about 40 years old with an attractive sleekness that Hollywood people aspire to acquire. Immaculately dressed, brimming with self-confidence and a tone of voice which was softly authoritative, she spelled things out.

"Doing commercials can be a career builder," she said. "There's a lot of work to go around, if you're interested." She ran through a partial list of her clients. There were numerous actors' names I recognized.

She gave me a long, searching look. "In this business," she said, "we try to find a niche for an actor, some particular type of character you can play again and again." In the old days, they'd call this typecasting and sometimes that could spell doom for an actor's career. If the character's popularity fell because the actor was identified with a single type of character, audiences wouldn't accept the actor in any other role.

With commercials, though, that didn't seem to matter. Screen time was short and the commercial highlighted not the actor as much as the product.

"I see you as the wholesome, clean-cut, executive type, outdoorsy but not a nut about it," she said. "You wouldn't be appropriate for heavy or trouble-making roles...."

And in that moment, we had found my niche in the world of television commercials. I suppose I could have found another niche: let my hair grow, for example, so it became scraggly, grow a grubby beard and assume a more threatening appearance. But I had to admit that really wasn't me, and I wasn't sure I'd enjoy playing that role, anyway. I felt most comfortable in my clean-cut, actor's persona, and agreed with Sonjia Brandon.

Soon, the roles began to come my way. Sonjia would call and say, "There's a commercial at so-and-so casting agency, and you need to get over there." The commercials would often be cast in a large room in an office building. When I'd arrive, there would be 50 actors similar to me, all capable of fitting the role in the commercial.

After going on a few of these calls, I got to know some of those guys who showed up because we were chasing the same roles. After some initial uncertainty, we found comfort in being around each other. We may have been rivals but if there was animus in the air, I sure didn't sense it.

I'd walk in and there would be the casting people. They'd give you a script to read. If you were lucky, you could sneak an five extra minutes to become familiar with it. Then, they'd video you as you read the script. After that, it was, "Thank you. We'll contact your agent."

If they were interested, you'd hear something in a matter of days. Often, it was a brief message from your agent who might tell you, "They want you on a call-back." That meant you had less competition and another shot at getting the role.

The next time you walked in the casting room, there were only ten or so guys called back, and chances were you knew most of them. But the audition didn't take place in the open, in front of the others.

"Follow me," an assistant producer would say and you'd find yourself in a separate room, with a script in your hand, reading before an audience of three or four, including the casting director.

Afterwards, you'd be directed to join the other actors outside the room and wait as each was called in individually. Once everyone had been auditioned, the casting director would join the actors and point to the ones who didn't make it. and You'd sit there, agonized before that moment, hoping they didn't call your name.

You soon realized that performing before the casting people was only the first step, that the production people were really the ones who called the shots. So, you got ready for the next round which would be with the director and producer only. Once again, you went into a separate room, this time with that audience of two.

Some intimacy would creep in. "Tell us about your acting background," they might say, or ask what commercials you'd appeared in, which directors or producers you might have worked with...

And after performing one last time, you went home and waited, and waited, trying not to get caught up in reviewing your performance, trying to remember any comments that could be construed as supportive.

And if you were chosen for the commercial, it felt like you won the lottery because it opened the door to making some serious money. If it was a national commercial, it would be shown across the country in every major market and seen by millions of television viewers. Depending upon how long the commercial stayed on the air, you could make upwards of $50,000 for one 30 second screen appearance.

The shoots generally lasted little more than a day, and the production team had it all planned out ahead of time. They knew what they wanted to do from one second to the next, often set out in a series of storyboards which were usually arrayed on easels, corresponding to the chronological progress of the commercial. The initial one might reference the first five seconds of air time, establishing the identity of characters, supers of product names, description of screen action, and so on. The next story board would pick things up from there, covering the next five seconds and continue with the story line. In this way the entire production would be laid out for cast and crew.

You generally got paid the minimum, whatever that amount was specified to be for that day under the existing production contract. But then came the best part, waiting to see if residuals came in. Each time the commercial aired, anywhere in the world, the actors received compensation based on the scale set forth in the standard production contract. If you had a hot commercial, the residuals grew and you could sit back and cash the checks.

When you did get hired or "booked," you got the same money whether you had a speaking role or not, so long as you appeared on screen. The exception was when you were a recognizable spokesperson for the particular product.

My first commercial was for Career Club shirts, a spiffy, European design that featured bold colors and vintage collars. I played a young guy sauntering along the street wearing his Career Club shirt, attracting the attention of lovely young women as he passed. Then, as the commercial neared the end, a furry, friendly dog appeared, and trotted after him, too. It was a 30 second shoot, over almost before it began, but somehow, my Career Club shirt relayed a message of inclusion, relevance and desire.

Call me shallow but was as important to me was the check that came along with the work. For the next 25 years, it formed an additional and welcome form of bread and butter survival.

I don't think an actor ever retired just by doing commercials, but there are situations where the amount of the payday can bring a broad smile to your face. For me, that happened when I was hired to perform in a Heinz ketchup commercial. The scene was a wooded campsite where my son and I settled for the night. We were making dinner and my son held a bottle of Heinz ketchup upside down, waiting for it to come out of the bottle.

"Dad," he said, "why won't the ketchup come out quicker?"

I responded with, "Son, if the ketchup came out any quicker, it wouldn't be Heinz."

Suddenly, there was alluring music, and Carly Simon began to sing "Anticipation." And my supposed son and I share smiles.

This commercial, in 21st century speak, went "viral," playing across the country and elsewhere, wherever Heinz products were available. I figured the residuals on that Heinz commercial alone through the years, earned me more than $100,000. I guess some things really are worth waiting for.

Something I liked about doing commercials was that you were often on location when doing them. Unlike standard movie and television development, where the production can often be done on a back lot in Hollywood and reconstituted to portray reality, commercials thrive on the freshness of a live scene because their screen time is so short and reality has to be instantaneous.

My location travels in the world of commercials gave me a chance to see places I might never have experienced, otherwise. For example, not long after wrapping the Heinz ketchup commercial, I was hired to do a Geritol commercial, and that one took me to Naples, Florida, somewhere I'd never been before. This commercial also did well, netting me about half of what the Heinz commercial paid. But when you're into the middle of five figures that's still a very nice payday for a day's work.

Then, I heard from the Pabst Blue Ribbon people, producers of the eponymous beer brand, in Milwaukee, Wisconsin. "We want to book you for two commercials," they said, "one now, one in a year." I never did get the rationale for the one year spread, but when the first check arrived, it was nice to know there would be another along eventually. That first Pabst commercial had me portray a sailor at sea, reveling in the refreshment of a cold, tingling brew while the sea winds blew and the blue water sparkled. It was a commercial that projected comfort and pleasure with an assist from Mother Nature.

A year later, it was "on location" with Pabst, as we arrived on the Big Island of Hawaii and landed near Hilo.

"We need a volcano for this shoot," one of the producers explained when I asked why we had come so far to produce it. Mind you, I wasn't complaining, I had never been to Hawaii and I was quite happy about the location. But after the producer's comment, I figured I'd keep things to myself and enjoy the many things the island had to offer. It did seem, though, that some producers and directors of commercials were no different than the rest of us: When the chance to get out of town crops up, they search for a location as far away from the office as possible.

And if that means traveling a couple of thousand miles, when other alternatives may be closer, so be it. In this case, they located a small, inactive volcano just outside Hilo, and decided it would do just fine.

I played a volcanologist, and the producers sent a special effects team to the bottom of the crater to set up a forced volcanic explosion that would be part of the on-screen story line. As the commercial began, I leaned over the crater edge and studied what appeared to be an active volcano. My volcanologist colleagues and I swilled beer (Pabst, of course), making notes on the suddenly exploding volcano and still enjoying our beer and not getting burned alive.

Occasionally, doing commercials did push the safety envelope, and unless you're a trained stuntman, you never feel that secure when doing it. I remember the early movie days at Universal when I was cocky enough to believe I could manage my own stunts, and then find, after painful and bloody bruising that there were those who could do it better and painlessly.

Sometimes, though, the question about whether you or the stuntman should do the action is close enough that you decide to take the chance yourself. This is what happened when I was booked for a Castrol commercial. The company, well-known in the auto and motorcycle culture for engine lubricants, had me on location in the desert, strolling along carrying a can of Castrol and verbally extolling the product while, whoosh, a car shot past, followed by another and another Ahead, the first car suddenly reversed and came roaring right back at me while the other cars peeled off in other directions, reversed and made straight for me as well. I continued my stroll and my happy words about Castrol. Then the first car slammed on its brakes just before running me over. Then the second car does the same, as does the third car, all of them now just inches away from crushing me. Of course, I acted like I was totally unaware of being moments away from my demise.

I had to hand it to these Hollywood stunt car drivers. They really knew what they were doing, reversing at full speed and stopping so suddenly and so close to me. Even now, as I think back to it, I get chills recalling how I maintained my cool through all of it, never flinching, never hesitating.

And also never ever doing it again.

Once in a while, I was able to get Helene and my two sons into a commercial, and the most memorable one was for Pizza Hut, the worldwide chain of restaurants. At first, the kids really loved the idea of free pizza, cooked to order. But after the third take, excitement faded and Helene and I could saw the fun of it all fast disappearing. By the fourth take, we knew something had to be done because the thought of consuming still another piece of pizza made us queasy.

After a quick family conference, we came up with a solution, namely pretend to eat the pizza, or at least appear to chew it. The instant the director said "cut" and the camera was off, we spit out the pizza and miserably got ready for the next piece.

We went on this way throughout the day. We pretended to happily eat pizza on camera, and then made horrible noises expelling it from our mouths when the cameras stopped.

Overall, I did well over one hundred commercials, and by the end of each one, I looked back with certain satisfaction at the quality of my work. But after a full day of shoving pizza in my face and nearly gagging while firing it out, I had trouble even saying the word over the next several months.

In the mid 1990s, my work in commercials began to slow down, and I wasn't called or booked with the regularity I once experienced. There were a number of things at play, including the fact I was getting older and less believable as a debonair, clean-cut, 30-something character behind the wheel of a spiffy sports car. I was now in late middle age, and roles in commercials for someone like me were not as plentiful as they were for someone younger. I began to wonder where my future with commercials would go.

I heard about a woman who had developed a niche market within the wider world of general commercials. Her name was Idell James, and she had created a market for what she called "background artists," which was Hollywood speak for commercial extras, people who appeared on camera, often as part of a crowd or in the background, with no lines or defined role, except as viewable wallpaper.

Idell was actually an agent. She was well-respected by producers and advertising agencies, and she had transformed the lowly role of the film extra into something actors could feel good about assuming. Calling yourself an extra in the film or television world was the most despised acting role in Hollywood, and you were treated like dog meat.

Idell turned all of this around by demanding that those working for her were serious actors, even though there were no lines to recite. Most importantly, you had to have your proper outfit. She might say, "We're going to work at the airport tomorrow. You'll need a suit and an attaché case." If you didn't appear with the proper outfit, or if you arrived late, you'd be fired on the spot. She expected you to be professional at all times.

"Day after tomorrow," she once said, "we'll be at a public swimming pool. So, make sure you have your swim suit and a towel handy." And by God, you had to have that stuff with you.

She might hear from the producers or advertising agencies, "We need one gray haired guy and three middle-aged women." She'd supply them, always referring to her actors as "background artists," which made you stand just a little straighter. At that time, I had gray hair, so I was one of those "older gray-haired guys" that supplied.

It was a long way from being the lead in a film. But gradually, working with her, you came to feel it was similar to being in a family.

"Where are we going this week?" I would ask. The weeks filled up steadily, and I was cast regularly.

You never did much traveling with this type of work, but the world of the background artist wasn't a big world, and you encountered the same actors and directors again and again. The familiarity could sometimes even add to your income.

A director came up and said, "Yeah, we did some work on a commercial last year. How are things going?"

And I responded that things were a little slow, so he nodded and said, "Okay, on this shoot, I want you to sit over there," and he pointed to a spot and added, "You're reading the paper and when the girl comes by, I'll come in close on you and you give her a wink."

It was called "giving" me the commercial. Because he arranged it so that I had a close-up and some specific stage business, I got an upgrade which entitled me to residuals for as long as the commercial was on the air. This actually happened quite a bit. Sometimes, the director was kind enough to insert a single, innocuous line for me to say, like, "How're you doing today?"

Other times, I might just walk across the set with the camera following me in a close-up. I might have the camera stay on me momentarily with a long shot as I harangued a crowd or went through a physical exercise.

The point of it all was that you were an extra until you weren't. The moment your character's individuality showed on screen, you went from background artist to something more. I'll never forget that even though folks knew I had seen better days in my career, they did their best to improve my lot.

Chapter Fourteen

Saved by the Bill

My background artist work with Idell James was never steady. There were weeks when I'd yearn for the phone to ring and nothing happened. Then, suddenly, there would be work, but sometimes, for a few weeks only. It was the mid 1990s and opportunities in the acting business were becoming limited.

It wasn't just me. Some of my friends suffered from this slump as well, and it meant we had to look outside the profession to find a steady check. Pride, of course, is something you have to toss away at the door when you're faced with this choice. The only comfort you could take was the certain knowledge that legions of actors before you had gone through the same thing and found work that bore no relation to their innate acting skills.

For me, this meant signing up to sell time shares, which I hated, figuring it was more scam than honest commerce. I was forced to cold-call to find investors for low-budget films produced by friends, which was not my cup of tea, either.

Finally, I turned to a fellow actor who also had a tree cutting and disposal business.

"Sure, but you won't get rich," he warned when I approached him, "I can pay you what I pay the Mexican kids I hire."

It turned out to be some of the toughest work I've ever done. I'd stay on the ground with the chain saw, and my friend would be up in the trees, cutting limbs and letting them drop to the ground. I cut the fallen limbs down in size and then loaded them into the truck, while my friend continued his work with the top branches. Do this work for an hour and you'd feel it that night.

Do it for half a day or longer, and you'll ache for a week. But at least I was getting a check, and from time to time, I'd get a call from Idell James for background artist work, so the tree cutting was endurable, though barely.

This back and forth between tree cutting and background artist work went on for over a year, and I could feel myself growing restive with both. I was in my sixties. A lot of acting years had gone by, and while I had had a satisfying and occasionally exciting career, I wasn't sure about what my acting future would be. As for the tree cutting, the physical demands were hardly getting easier, and the chance of serious injury always was present when I operated the chainsaw.

I found myself yearning for a life of greater peace and tranquility. I had a vision of finding a quiet island in Maine where Helene and I could slip into a world of comfortable anonymity with woods and mountains and seashore nearby, with privacy and small town contentment to surround us. So I did some research and found there were realtors dotted along the Maine coast who were glad to help. Referrals and brochures came in the mail, and Helene and I began a search for what we hoped would be a retirement location.

I still did my background artist work, though I figured those days were numbered. I was hired to appear in a rodeo setting for a Dodge truck commercial. We were in an arena, standing around a Dodge truck. I was a cowboy-rodeo performer. Next to me, slouched against the truck, was Tim McGee, a *real* cowboy and actor who owned a big ranch nearby. Thin, weathered and soft-spoken, Tim found time to chat with me during filming breaks. At one point, he looked me up and down, and said, "You'd make a good Buffalo Bill. They're always looking for the right guy for that gig."

I had no idea what he was talking about, and it must have showed because he laughed and clapped me on the shoulder. "I'm talking about the Disney folks and their big deal operation in Paris."

He was referring to Euro Disney (now Disneyland Paris), the recently opened, highlyanticipated amusement park, specially keyed to European tastes. "They do a Buffalo Bill act, most every day," he said, adding he'd worked on the show for three years, and the search for people to play Buffalo Bill was constant. Why Buffalo Bill, I wondered? Why would such an American icon make sense in a European setting? McGee gave me a quick history lesson. In the 1880s and 1890s there was Buffalo Bill's Wild West Show, featuring Indians such as Sitting Bull and famed buffalo hunter William Cody, which toured Europe year after year and brought fame and notoriety for decades. Euro Disney was recreated the experience for a new generation.

"Can you ride?" McGee asked me.

"I'm no expert," I admitted.

"Can you *sit* on a horse is what I mean?"

I nodded. "I know what it feels like."

McGee said the Euro Disney people were coming to his ranch in Malibu in a few days, looking for a new Buffalo Bill.

"Why don't you come out and give it a shot?" he suggested. "I'll get you a horse. You can meet the producer and director. I'll even get you the lines so you can practice them." He also suggested I come out a couple of days ahead of time so I could familiarize myself with the horse and with what it felt like to be back in the saddle. "Get the feel of it," was the way he put it.

And I took him up on it, more out of curiosity than desire. Playing Buffalo Bill, living and working in Paris, riding a horse and being paid for it every day. I wondered if it was more fantasy than reality. But it sure did beat tree cutting.

Then the day of the audition arrived, and when I showed up at the ranch, it was clear I had competition. I counted ten other middle-aged, gray-haired men, moving around the horses and the film crew. That's when reality hit: It would be like any other audition. There was a director to call the shots, and you'd be expected to follow his instructions. Only this time, I had to convince a horse to cooperate.

I'd done my homework, and when I was called, I climbed on the horse, as gracefully as I could, did my lines with as much verve as I could manage and finished off by galloping right up to the camera, coming to a sudden, well-disciplined stop and tried to act as if it was something I did every day.

I left the audition feeling pretty good about things, but as the days dragged along and I didn't hear from them, I began to think it just hadn't worked out. Sadly, you get used to that in this business. So Helene and I turned back to our plans for a retirement move to the east coast.

"It's off to Maine!" Helene announced more than once, and I usually responded with, "I guess," because somewhere, deep down, I couldn't erase the remaining bit of desire to perform in Paris.

About a month after the audition, Helene and I were packing our final bags and tracing our route back East on a big map when the phone rang.

"You got it!" came an excited voice with a French accent. "They want you as Buffalo Bill." And just like that, my privately held dream came true. I would mount a beautiful white horse, flash my natural and manicured white beard, wave my hat to a wildly cheering crowd and gallop to the middle of the arena, as an excited, French public address announcer shouted, *"Voici, Boooffaalo Beeeel!"*

It turned out that the reason for delay in getting back to me was because I had not been first choice for the role. That went to an actor whose wife was a Hollywood-based theatrical agent. She had pressed the French producers for a private vehicle, a driver, special hotel accommodations and a host of other perks. The French executives who were running things at Euro Disney weren't comfortable with this over-the-top Hollywood style and quickly cut off negotiations. They decided they didn't need the headaches and called the next guy on the list.

And that happened to be me.

But it wasn't simply, "You're hired" and then you perform.

I was told, "We need you in Paris, but you have to come alone. We want to put you through some tests to see how you'd do in the arena."

And within a couple of days of the phone call, I was on my way to France. They set me up in a dormitory right near the Euro Disney facility, and I began daily training for the Buffalo Bill Wild West Show. I worked with French trainers who were very strict. They were always on top of me to "get it right," down to the last detail of where I stood, how I sat the horse, and how I interacted with the other performers.

There was a probationary period of three months when I trained rigorously with the other horsemen, learned lines, got to know my horse and became familiar with the stage business I was expected to follow, once in the arena. It turned out that Michael Eisner, then head of Disney, had always wanted to do a Buffalo Bill Wild West Show and had built a dinner theater that could hold over 1000 patrons. He perched it right next to Euro Disney and added continental style restaurants so the dinner guests could enjoy international cuisine while watching the show.

In the beginning, I had trouble getting my cues right, where I should stop my horse, how I held myself as Bill and so on. But I was in luck. My horse was a Buffalo Bill Show veteran. He'd learned which cues were coming long before I had arrived on the scene, and that made it a lot easier. Sometimes, though, he'd just get impatient and want to move before his cue, and when that happened, it was a tough day, because I'd have to work hard to restrain him. Remember, he was 1200 pounds and I was a little less than that.

His name was *Carido*, meaning Sweetheart, and generally, we got along well because I always had an apple in my pocket when I first approached him each day. He'd see me and immediately start nickering, and when I got close enough, he'd sniff all my pockets until he located the apple. Then, I'd give it to him.

The show required a lot of precision, and it was complicated because performers playing Annie Oakley and Sitting Bull were also part of it. They came out and we interacted. There was a chase scene involving a stagecoach getting attacked by Indians, and I appeared suddenly, riding in on my big white horse and ultimately saved the day. It required a lot of timing and rehearsal to get the show right. We finally got it down and Helene and I moved to France. It was always a bit of a challenge, though, training with my horse before the show, going in for the latest costume fitting, learning my lines, especially the lines in French, which they changed without much warning now and then.. Generally, I worked two shows a day, and by the end, I dragged myself home and hopped in a big, warm tub.

A key part of the show was getting the audience to participate in what was happening on the arena floor. The Disney people provided each member of the audience with a colored cowboy hat, matching the color of the theater section where they sat. There were four separate sections and the performers formed teams under a given color and competed against one another in events such as barrel racing and stagecoach racing, with the audience cheering them on.

My role, once I had whipped the audience into a mild frenzy with my galloping out, was to work with the characters playing Annie Oakley and Sitting Bull. We set up a shooting contest when audience members came down to the stage and tried to best Annie Oakley, while Sitting.

Bull prowled the stage, looking fearsome. We made sure that any audience members we invited on stage included a little boy.

And then we'd make sure he'd win and be acclaimed as the one who "beat" Annie Oakley. The crowd always loved it.

Our cowboys and Indians came mostly, from the United States and Canada, and were not just a bunch of actors made up to look like cowboys and Indians. I remembered Tim McGee, who had set me up for the Buffalo Bill role. He oozed authenticity, lean, grizzled. It was no surprise that he owned horses as well as a working ranch and had spent three years doing a cowboy gig for Euro Disney.

At any one time, there were about 25 cowboys and 25 Indians in the cast, as well as 10 *live* buffalo which would be chased around the arena by the Indians, simulating a hunting expedition. At times, it could get a bit raucous because there was no way to script the buffalo. While repeated performances toned down their wilder instincts, they were hardly tame animals.

Occasionally, one or more broke away from the herd and searched for a way out of the arena.

The trainers were very skilled, though, and always on their toes in case animal discipline broke down.

As one of the trainers told me, "These are wild animals. You can't train them like a dog or cat. You do the best you can with what they give you."

A show like this, with its huge cast, numerous animals and precision story telling, is a massive challenge. It is not easy to achieve a problem-free production. Things happen. Sometimes bad things happen, when there's a cast of hundreds interacting with large animals, while thousands cheer and heavy music thumps and blasts. Just as with my Buffalo Bill character, the parts of Annie Oakley and Sitting Bull were not always played single performer. Actors playing these roles would eventually tire of it and want to move on. I lasted more than four years and over 1000 performances before my age and the job's physical demands got to me. So, periodically, there were new faces taking over these roles.

One replacement was Lisa Butler who came in to play Annie Oakley. Lisa was an accomplished actress, and she'd auditioned for the Annie Oakley role because it was unlike anything else she'd ever done. "An unusual challenge" was how she put it, and she did love challenges.

One particular evening, the show was winding down and word had come that one of our longest-performing Indians would be leaving the cast. It was my job as titular head of the show to announce to the audience if a cast member was leaving. I would do this just before we'd make our final exit. We were gathering, cast members and horses, near the exit, moving slowly offstage, and I flicked on my microphone button.

"Ladies and Gentlemen," I boomed and I announced the name of the cast member who was leaving and mentioned his years of service to the show. "Let's give him a big round of applause!" I encouraged, and the audience enthusiastically complied, sending waves of happy sound our way.

Then, on cue, the cowboys, all 25 of them, shouted "Yippee!" and threw their hats in the air to commemorate the send-off.

It was a routine we'd done many times, without a problem, and the audience always cheered along with us.

Only this time, it didn't end well. We were bunched along a concrete wall just outside the arena exit. One of the thrown cowboy hats unexpectedly brushed the face of the horse Lisa Butler was riding.

And her horse jumped and bucked and threw her head first into that concrete wall. For a long moment, there was utter silence in the arena. No one dared move, yet everyone stared down at the inert body of Lisa Butler on the arena floor.

Then, slowly, fearfully, the arena came to life. Medical personnel raced towards Lisa and within seconds, they were administering to her.

It turned out that the trauma of hitting that concrete wall with her head paralyzed Lisa from the neck down, but only temporarily.

Within a few weeks, she began to get feeling in her extremities and gradually, after several months, she regained all the feeling she had lost.

But the lesson was not lost on us. From that point forward, no hats were ever again tossed in the air, at least when the horses were nearby.

After I'd been on the show awhile, I realized I'd acquired the Buffalo Bill look. My moustache and beard had grown in naturally white and full, and with my lean face and proper beard trimming, I closely resembled my 19th century model. Helene and I had found a charming French village about a half an hour outside Paris, and we bought a small house there. I commuted to work by train, and with the steady drumbeat of Euro Disney publicity that included my photo as Buffalo Bill, it was impossible to go about and not get recognized. I'd hear snatches of whispered conversations with murmurs of "Buuuuuffallo Beeeel." I saw people pointing, nudging their neighbors and trying not to stare.

It could get a bit unnerving, I suppose, but I kept reminding myself that an actor, a performer, wants people to recognize him or her.

So, I strived to smile and not get caught up in the sociability of it.

There were times, though, when meeting the public outside the arena as Buffalo Bill was part of my job. Sometimes, after the afternoon show, word from the production team would filter down. "Stay in costume. Meet and greet in the park." And that meant that we'd move onto the theme park grounds, next door, and join with other costumed Disney characters such as Mickey Mouse and Goofy and Donald Duck for a session with the public. I'd be on my horse with Annie Oakley and Sitting Bull and our cast of cowboys and Indians nearby, and we'd line up so the fans could take photos, and pretend, for just a moment, that we were the real thing.

Sometimes, we'd get questions.

"Where are you really from?"

"How do I get a dream job like this?"

"They pay you well?" We'd make it a point to avoid responding to questions like those, merely showing a smile and a nod, never exhibiting an ounce of irritability or impatience. This was Disney, after all.

To add to the public's pleasure at seeing us in costume, I, as did the other costumed characters, always carried a raft of photos. I'd hand them out to anyone who'd want one, kids especially, always autographing them with, "Good luck! Buffalo Bill."

Working with the French turned out to be a delight. Our show was actually run by a French company under a licensing agreement with the Disney Corporation. The French company paid Disney a fee to use the Disney name and for the right to use the Disney characters, but on a day-to-day basis, the French company ran things. The French weren't snobbish or crabby or difficult to get along with. While they did get a bit touchy and prideful, perhaps even arrogant, over how French culture would be displayed in the midst of the Disney production, it never interfered with my working with them.

A lingering memory that will forever remain is the day we did the show on September 11, 2001. At the close of the afternoon Buffalo Bill Wild West Show, I learned of the horrific suicide attacks in New York City and Washington DC, and I realized I had another show to do that evening. We couldn't ignore what had happened We *had* to say something to the audience now and be ready to say more about it at the evening show.

The French director agreed with me. "Jeeem," he said, "you do it in English, and I will follow in French."

I walked to the center of the arena, still in costume, and spoke: "My friends," I said, a mixture of sadness and anger in my voice, "we must tell you what America has suffered this day." And I described what had happened, where it happened and who had done it.

The French director walked up, hugged me briefly, gave me a thumbs up and took the microphone. "*Mesdames et messieurs...*" he began.

Americans have many opinions about the French, but on that day, the world was on the side of the United States of America. We should remember that too, as well as the loss of life, and strive to be loved again for what we represent to the world.

Epilogue

IN 2002, I decided to hang up my Buffalo Bill spurs. I was 66 years old, the work was hard, and my aching body was telling me it was time to move on. It had been a wonderful adventure, but now we were ready to return home.

We came back to the Jersey shore where Helene had spent her summers, though she lived the rest of the year in Philadelphia. We were greeted by family and a ton of old friends. My mind was still fresh, so the idea of "retirement" was barely a blip on my radar scope; I wanted to stay active, and I turned to my art for creative fulfillment. Next to the house was a garage which I converted into a studio. I could work there without anyone dictating what to do or when to do it. The sense of freedom filled me with excitement.

About the same time, our son Tysun moved to the mountains east of Bakersfield, California, and when we visited him there, we fell in love with the area. It was about 4000 feet above sea level, quiet and serene, wooded and very rural. It had a calming, spiritual quality.

So, we bought a small cabin there, and suddenly, Helene and I realized, we were now "bicoastal." We'd spend our summers at the New Jersey shore, where the social life and the sailing were active and rewarding. We'd spend our winters in the California mountains, where I'd chop wood for heat. We'd live a rustic life about three hours east of Los Angeles and feel the tranquility that mountain privacy provides.

At the same time, I also knew that if I wanted to go back to acting, I could get down to Los Angeles easily because in the back of my mind there was the thought that maybe, just maybe, I'd give it all one more shot.

Friends often ask, now that I've been a way from it for awhile, whether I miss the show biz life. I'm really not sure. But to be frank, I think I'd like to try it one more time. It's a tough choice, though. In New Jersey, we're an hour and a half from New York City, and it's a drag to go in there and audition, again and again. In the mountains out west, we're even further from the action and auditions present the same problems. Also, I'd need to get an agent and a place to stay in Los Angeles and be available for those one-after-another auditions.

So, am I motivated to do all of that?

In 2017, I noted Robert Redford was going to perform in his final career movie, and of course I had worked with him on *Downhill Racer*, one of his first movies. I thought, what if we could connect one last time and close the circle? I got in touch with my old agent and got a copy of the script for the proposed movie which Redford was calling *The Old Man and the Gun*. Then I spoke with Redford, and after we caught each other up on our lives, he said, "We haven't done the casting yet. When we do, I'll call you, and you can meet the director and producer. We'll take it from there."

After the call, I admit I was excited, and plans for a late-blooming acting career began to form in my head. What would be my next role after *this* movie?

Sadly, it never happened. Destiny raised its ugly head in the form of the big C, cancer, and suddenly I had to undergo eight weeks of radiation which effectively doomed my chances to reunite with Redford. I called his office to let them know.

My contact in his office said, "No problem. This may be his final movie as an actor, but he doesn't plan to stop directing or producing movies. There'll be lots of chances ahead."

And that's where I am in my late career acting life. Because, you see, I'm really curious to see what is next. It's curiosity that brings you adventures. It's curiosity that helps you fully explore your creativity. It's curiosity that keeps the mind alive.

www.ingramcontent.com/pod-product-compliance
Lightning Source LLC
Chambersburg PA
CBHW051051160426
43193CB00010B/1145